Discovering God:
Life's Adventure

John M. Scott, S.J.

Our Sunday Visitor Publishing Division
Our Sunday Visitor, Inc.
Huntington, Indiana 46750

ISBN: 0-87973-429-9
LCCCN: 91-66662

PRINTED IN THE UNITED STATES OF AMERICA

Cover design by Rebecca J. Heaston

429

*Dedicated to my friends
who help make God "so real" to me*

ACKNOWLEDGMENTS

The author and publisher wish to express their thanks to those individuals (or their representatives, agents, or estates) and publishers who have given permission to make use of their materials in this work. Among them are Barbara Beckwith, Dr. Wernher von Braun, Father Walter J. Burghardt, S.J., Jack Horkheimer, James B. Irwin, Father James Hart McCown, S.J., Father William J. Menster, H. V. Morton, Dr. Kathleen M. O'Connor, Father William J. O'Malley, S.J., Father John Powell, S.J., Sister Rose Michael Weber, Virginia Lanphier, Helen Steiner Rice, Barbara Tippery, and Father William J. Menster; special thanks go to the *Omaha World-Herald*, Gibson Greeting Cards, Inc., Harper and Row Publishers, Inc., and Loyola University Press. If any copyrighted materials have been inadvertently used in this book without proper credit being given in one manner or another, please notify Our Sunday Visitor in writing so that future printings of this work may be corrected accordingly.

CONTENTS

1

How to Find God

You don't have to cruise three hundred eighty miles above the earth and peer through the $1.5-billion Hubble Space Telescope to find God.

Elizabeth Barrett Browning reminded us that every common bush is afire with God. Too many people, alas, do not see the flame. They simply stand around and pluck blackberries.

For centuries no one dreamed that ordinary "white" light is made up of all the colors of the rainbow. Then along came Sir Isaac Newton. He placed a prism in the path of a beam of light, and behold the magic, which you can duplicate for yourself. The prism breaks up the beam of light into a spectrum of dazzling colors.

The prism we need to show us that God is present in the world all around us is the prism of wonder.

Listen to Albert Einstein describe how wonder can lead to God: "The most beautiful thing we can experience is the mysterious. It is the source of all true art and science. He to whom this emotion is a stranger, who can no longer pause to wonder and stand rapt in awe, is as good as dead; his eyes are closed.

"This insight into the mystery of life has also given rise to religion. To know that what is impenetrable to us really exists, manifesting itself as the highest wisdom and the most radiant beauty which our dull faculties can comprehend only in their most primitive forms — this knowledge, this feeling, is the center of true religiousness."

Dag Hammarskjöld would have us keep in mind that "we die on the day when our lives cease to be illumined by the steady radiance, renewed daily, of a wonder, the source of which is beyond all reason."

According to Pierre Teilhard de Chardin, each person's task is to perceive God hidden in the heart of the universe, to utter the words of consecration over all the elements, toils, and labors of this world so that everything becomes part of the cosmic Christ.

In words vibrating with enthusiasm and joy, Father Teilhard de Chardin exclaims, "Lord, it is you who, through the imperceptible goadings of sense-beauty, penetrated my heart in order to make its life flow out into yourself.

"You came down into me by means of a tiny scrap of created reality; and then, suddenly, you unfurled your immensity before my eyes and displayed yourself to me.

"In the life springing up within me, in the material elements that sustain me, it is not just your gifts that I discern; it is you yourself that I encounter, you who cause me to share in your own being, and whose hands mould me."

Father John Catoir tells us, "To delight in the Lord we need a little imagination, a loving spirit and most of all the faith to see God as a personal lover present and working in every aspect of our lives. He is present to each of us in a personal way.

"As a flawed human being myself, I marvel that this sense of closeness to God is given to me. I've learned that if I focus on myself, on my own sinfulness, I'm lost. The key is to concentrate on the Lord, to love Him and love what He loves."

According to the Jesuit poet Father Gerard Manley Hopkins:

The world is charged with the grandeur of God,
Because the Holy Ghost over the bent
World broods with warm breast and with ah! bright
 wings.

To Wonder Is Natural

We are born to wonder. When we allow this gift to atrophy, even if we are young in years, we are already more than half in love with easeful death.

Everything important begins with wonder. Learning and great art stand on the acknowledgment that the air we inhale, the moon, the sea, and the sun, laughter, and the love of friends are not human rights but divine gifts.

"To wonder at creation," says Hugh Lavery, "is man's true calling. Human inventiveness is not original; originality belongs to God. The great artist is always aware that he does not know where his best insights come from, that the spark he calls inspiration is not struck of common flint, that his work is revelation of a reality already there, but unnoticed, unexplored. The artist does not create; he reveals. The real artistic gift is the gift of wonder.

"Every child wonders, and feeds on surprise. The dawn of wonder is the first dawn of divinity."

In his fascinating, inspiring book *Vital Spiritualities*, published in 1990, Father Gerard T. Broccolo urges us to become aware of the presence of God in everyday life. If we do, we will want to proclaim with the psalmist: "It is good to give thanks to the Lord, to make music to your name, O Most High, to proclaim your love in the morning and your truth in the watches of the night, on the ten-stringed lyre and the lute, with the murmuring sound of the harp. Your deeds, O Lord, have made me glad; for the work of your hands, I shout with joy. How deep are your designs!" (Psalm 92).

The simplest works of nature proclaim the grandeur of the universe and the miracle of life. Nature's simple beauty whispers softly in the heart. Each corner of the world, no matter how plain and simple, has a story to tell: a story of beauty, of blessed loveliness, a poem without words. Ceaselessly traveling through time, each soul seeks its golden moment.

How precious our moments of quiet communion with the world when the soul reawakens to the wonder of life! Sometimes a message reaches us through our eyes; a message of simple truth, accompanied by warmth and sympathy, reaches us without words, in total silence. We stop and look, and everything stands still, everything but the beauty before us. And we hear a poem without words.

I love to recall the opening prayer of the Mass I said at Patch Grove, Wisconsin, on the morning of July 24, 1977: "God, our Father, open our eyes to see your hand at work in the splendor of creation. Touched by your hand our world is holy. Help us to cherish the gifts that surround us."

According to Rabbi Alexander M. Schindler, we should "never be too busy for the wonder and the awe of life. Be reverent before each dawning day. Embrace each hour. Seize each golden minute."

Religion Begins in Wonder

A group of Catholic educators meeting in Washington, D.C., were told, "There is religion in the world because we have the capacity to wonder."

Sister Bernadette O'Connell, assistant director of the Family Life Bureau of the Archdiocese of Philadelphia, has created a religious-education program to help parents realize that they can build a child's awareness of a "wonder-full" God.

The key to this whole development, according to Sister Bernadette, is the notion of wonder itself. All discovery begins in wonder. She calls wonder "the natural religious sense."

"As children stand in wonder of God's work," she says, "as they see people and the world as good, they seek to know who made it all."

Religion has been defined as a deep awareness of God as the basis of all things. It is a response to reality apprehended as divine. When God is seen everywhere, there is two-way communication, and perhaps that is the highest form of worship.

Religious educators strongly emphasize that moral formation is a response to one's relationship with God. At the very heart of the process is the concept of wonder. Sister Bernadette calls it "the link between the human area and the spiritual — that which gives a whole extra dimension to life, that which conditions people to appreciate the details of life."

Some people have the unfortunate habit of looking upon religion as restricting or limiting our lives. In reality, it fosters growth.

"A mind focused on God's wonder," says Vincent P. Small, "is a mind in action, speculating, playing with concepts, in short creating. Such a mind will be less easily stifled — not only in its quest for God, but in its quest for everything! Such a mind will surely be a spur to growth."

'You Cease to Be an Exile. . .'

In the summer of 1987 a remarkable man by the name of Father Anthony de Mello died. A Jesuit priest from India, he awakened in countless listeners a sense of wonder that is essential to being fully human. "You cease to be an exile when you discover that creation is your home," he would say.

According to Father de Mello, our experiences of living in this world should help us feel drawn to a lasting union with God.

Helen Steiner Rice reminds us that "God's miracles are all around within our sight and touch and sound."

Walt Whitman asks:

Why, who makes much of a miracle?
As to me, I know of nothing else but miracles,
Whether I walk the streets of Manhattan,
Or dart my sight over the roofs of houses toward the
    sky,
Or wade with naked feet along the beach just on the
    edge of the water,
Or stand under the trees in the woods.
To me every hour of the light and dark is a miracle,
Every cubic inch of space is a miracle,
Every square yard of the surface of the earth is spread
    with the same,
Every foot of the interior swarms with the same.

Philosopher Gerald Heard once described wonder as "that mixture of profound awe and overwhelming self-forgetful delight which is the true catharsis and deliverance of the soul."

The Quaker mystic Rufus Jones wrote, "The human heart is sensitive to God as the retina is to light waves."

According to Ardis Whitman, worship can never be confined to the walls of church or temple, for it is an attitude toward life, a response to the universe around us. The essence of worship is wonder.

Ardis then goes on to say, "It is not surprising that heaven comes down to touch us when we find ourselves safe in the heart of another person. Human love is like the shine of gold in the prospector's pan — so different from its surroundings that it seems we must have found it in a better world. 'After you had taken your leave,' wrote the Indian philosopher Rabindranath Tagore to a beloved guest, 'I found God's footprints on my floor.' "

The poet Bradford Smith, aware that he was soon to die of cancer, watched dawn breaking over the eastern horizon and wrote:

Oh, God, how beautifully you light your world!
With what majestic sweetness the light comes on.

We need Smith's sense of awe and gratitude to rekindle within us a reverence for life. He teaches us to cherish the wonders of the universe.

'Beauty Seen Is Never Lost'

Because I walked to the bottom of the Grand Canyon, I know something of the majesty and grandeur of God; because I climbed snow-capped Alps, I know something of the dazzling, breathtaking splendor of God; because I have watched the sun, and moon, and stars in their ponderous courses, I know something of his power and skill.

Tennyson reminds us, "Beauty seen is never lost. God's colors all are fast. The glory of the sunset heaven into my soul has passed."

And Hazel Simon says:

There are vast silences yet, without words,
There is a language in each quiet place,
On every work of God is written, "Love."
And every lake reflects His kindly face.

English journalist and author Beverly Nichols in his autobiography, *All I Could Never Be*, tells us how he came to God: "It was inevitable, I suppose, that in the garden I should begin, at long last, to ask myself what lay behind all this beauty. When guests were gone, and I had the flowers to myself, I was so happy that I wondered why at the same time I was haunted by a sense of emptiness. It was as though I wanted to thank somebody, but had nobody to thank; which is another way of saying that I felt the need for worship. That is, perhaps, the kindliest way in which a man may come to his God."

The poet Molly Anderson Haley reminds us:

I never knew Thee, Lord, until
My garden brought us face to face,
Revealed Thy gracious miracle
Of sun, and seed in little space,
Since I have seen Thine alchemy
Change earth-brown bulb to living gold
Of daffodils, eternity
Has seemed a simple truth to hold.

Like the old master painter in the faraway hills who pours out his heart in a symphony of color to tell his love and devotion, the Master Painter etches the story of his love for us in every flower and blossom.

Meet God in Your Garden

Phyllis Theroux tells us how she met God in her garden: "It all began with a plot of earth and a packet of seeds. I felt a contained excitement jacketed like a seed within the soil. Looking at that brown raked square, laid out with string, I realized that I was nothing more than a custodian to a mystery beyond my comprehension.

"I think this is what hooks one on gardening; it is the closest one can come to being present at the Creation."

Louis M. Savery reminds us that "by faith we perceive that the universe was fashioned by the word of God so that the visible came forth from the invisible. (Hebrews 11:3) Once God is present within, a new century begins. The world changes its skin, a new geography has to be charted, new doors and windows open up, and God is found in all the things that have been made.

"The inward eye is opened and sees everything new, under the light of the Spirit. Everything seems fresh and holy. There is a passion for experience, a longing to see and touch things, to meet the whole world with love. This world seems to become ever more rich and personal. Most of all, to the person who searches for God everywhere, the world is a challenge. Everywhere he turns, in everything he touches, he may discover something about God. The believer who allows himself to be enveloped by God can smile, can laugh, can cry with happiness. All things are new. The kingdom of God is at hand."

The Wonders of Life

One of my former students, Douglas Mainor, joined the Navy after finishing high school. In his first letter to me he wrote, "Last week for the first time I went out to sea. It was beautiful to see the dawn as the sun rose in the glory of God, spewing forth golden beams like a thousand rainbows spun of gold. I'll never forget my first time out. I saw the sea at peace. In the future I'll also see it in all its power."

The mother of fourteen children wrote to describe the greatest wonders in her life:

I have looked upon the flowers,
I have gazed at towering trees,
I've marveled at the mountain peaks,
And I've seen the mighty seas.
But no beauty in the universe
Or wonder on the earth
Can be as great a miracle
As the mystery of birth.
Each life becomes a masterpiece,
Each soul a breath from above.
All have a special destiny.
All are made for His love.

The one saint who, above all others, made use of his gift of wonder to approach God was St. Francis of Assisi. The attitude of St. Francis toward creation is beautifully illustrated by Barbara Beckwith in her inspiring article that appeared in the October 1982 issue of *St. Anthony Messenger*. With joy I acknowledge my gratitude to Barbara for permission to share her insights with you.

What can Francis teach us about nature? After all, in the 800 years since his birth we have learned much about biology, botany, human and veterinary medicine, the earth sciences, evolution. But in many ways we seem to have proceeded without incorporating the basic reverential approach espoused by St. Francis. What precisely was his attitude toward creation?

Francis saw in all creation an expression of God. "In everything beautiful, he saw Him who is beauty itself, and he followed his Beloved everywhere by his likeness imprinted on creation; all of creation he made a ladder by which he might mount up and embrace Him who is all desirable," says St. Bonaventure.

Francis could become absorbed in prayer while holding a small waterfowl in his hands, "rejoicing over it in the Lord." All nature was for him sanctified by the Incarnation. Jesus was here; he made the universe holy.

Like the English mystical poet William Blake, Francis "could see heaven in a wildflower."

In the broad sense, a sacrament is a sign or symbol of a spiritual reality. Thus, nature functioned for Francis as a sacrament of God's goodness. Thomas of Celano notes that Francis "rejoiced in all the works of the hands of the Lord and saw behind things pleasant to behold their life-giving reason and cause."

Francis is "the man of wonder" according to Eloi Leclerc, O.F.M., in *The Song of Dawn*. "He possessed an exceptional capacity to be amazed." The very words used to describe his feelings — rejoicing, delight, gratitude, a wonderful and ineffable joy — connote wonder. "When he considered the glory of the flowers, how happy he was to gaze at the beauty of their forms and to enjoy their marvelous fragrance," Celano says of him. Could St. Francis have originated the admonition "Take time to smell the roses"?

Francis believed that every creature proclaims, "God made me for your sake, O man," thus acknowledging the preeminence of the human in the scheme of creation.

Francis "called all creatures brother, and in a most extraordinary manner, a manner never experienced by others, he discerned the hidden nature of things with his sensitive heart, as one who had already escaped into the freedom of the glory of the sons of God," says Celano.

Nowhere is this tendency to see the relatedness of all Creation better expressed than in Francis' "Canticle of Brother Sun," where sun, wind and fire are addressed as brother, and moon, earth and death as sister — all elements of the universe bound together by the Fatherhood of God.

There is no sexism here; rather, the complementarity, the necessity, of the feminine is stressed. Armstrong argues that the creatures designated masculine are associated with power and robustness, the feminine ones with gentleness, and generosity, from a tradition dating back at least to classical mythology. Francis' recognition of the feminine as no less significant in God's scheme than the masculine — a sisterhood and brotherhood cooperating with one another — was remarkable for his time.

Many people in this last century have indeed caught the spirit of St. Francis.

Two Jesuits, one an Englishman who taught classics, the other a French scientist, ordained thirty years apart and separated by worlds of experience, came to adopt Francis' idea of the sacramentality of nature. Poet

17

Gerard Manley Hopkins, whose whole life was spent teaching in England and Ireland, took deep delight in "dappled things" and through them was led to see the Creator's hand: "He fathers-forth whose beauty is past change; Praise him." For him. . .

The world is charged with the grandeur of God.
It will flow out, like shining from shook foil.
It gathers to a greatness, like the ooze of oil
Crushed. Why do men then now not reck his rod?
Generations have trod, have trod, have trod. . .
And for all this, nature is never spent;
There lives the dearest freshness deep down
    things.

Père Pierre Teilhard de Chardin, who served as a stretcher-bearer in World War I and was in Peking, China, when atom bombs were dropped on Japan in 1945, was a geologist and paleontologist. He came to realize *The Divine Milieu* in the heart of matter: "This is what I have learned from my contact with the earth — the diaphaneity of the divine at the heart of a glowing universe, the divine radiating from the depths of matter a-flame."

Other scientists have shared Francis' sense of awe and wonder at "how fearfully we are made," how intricate all life is. Conservationist Peter Matthiesen has written that "we must feel awe again if we are ever to return to a harmonious existence with our habitat and survive."

That necessary sense of awe is well communicated by Dr. Lewis Thomas, who has taught at a number of medical schools and serves as president of the Sloan-Kettering Cancer Center in New York City. His lucid, witty, popular essays on biology (*Notes of a Biology Watcher*), collected in two volumes (*The Lives of a Cell* and *The Medusa and the Snail*), never take life for granted.

For example, in his comments *On Embryology*, Thomas says, "A short while ago, in mid-1978, the newest astonishment in medicine, covering all the front pages, was the birth of an English baby nine months after conception in a dish. The older surprise, which should still be fazing us all, is that a solitary sperm and a single egg can fuse and become a human being under any circumstance."

Jacques Cousteau is another who shared Francis' vision of all life as interlocked. Compassionate by nature for the sea creatures he encounters in his dives into their wet world, he records the sounds of whales and analyzes the chemistry of various waters.

Recently he and the crew of his boat *Calypso* undertook a study commissioned by a number of governments along the Mediterranean Sea which will help to rectify the sources of pollution affecting those waters.

The Franciscan virtue of compassion is also well exemplified by James Herriot, whose tales of veterinary medicine in the Yorkshire countryside (starting with *All Creatures Great and Small* through to *The Lord God Made Them All*, and now in TV episodes) have conveyed a real sympathy for animals.

In 1980 Pope John Paul II proclaimed the Assisian the patron saint of ecology, a sign to us that St. Francis' attitude is exactly what is needed today.

As our patron of ecology, no doubt St. Francis of Assisi continues to nudge people to notice Sister Moon, care for Brother Rabbit, and even to tolerate Cousin Pigeon — and through them come closer to God.

'A Cup of Blessing'

"Never lose an opportunity of seeing anything that is beautiful," urged Ralph Waldo Emerson, "for beauty is God's handwriting — a wayside sacrament. Welcome it in every fair face, in every fair sky, in every flower, and thank God for it as a cup of blessing."

Growing toward God can have something of the experience of exploration. It is like traveling the roaring waves of the sea in search of a land. It involves holding fast to dreams. It involves straining after the promise of the truly mysterious or it is like traveling beyond towering mountains to touch with your hands the loam of a hidden valley. More than this, it is like wanting to spin the dazzling universe in the palm of your hand.

Perhaps there has been a time in your life when for the moment there was an ineffable joy and exaltation. The experience was like the effect of some great orchestra when all the separate notes have melted into one swelling harmony that leaves you conscious of nothing save that your spirit is being wafted upward and almost bursting with your emotions.

Return to Wonder

Ardis Whitman urges us "to return to the wonder of the child. Seek the occasion and seize the day, as a child does. Rise before dawn some morning and see the miracle of creation all over again. Rise, too, at night, and see moonlight in the empty streets. Watch how the wind plays with the bright leaves of a maple tree in the spring."

"Use your eyes," wrote Helen Keller, "as if tomorrow you would be stricken blind; hear the music of voices, the song of a bird, as if you would be stricken deaf tomorrow. Touch each object as if tomorrow your tactile sense would fail. Smell the perfume of flowers, taste with relish each morsel, as if tomorrow you could never smell and taste again."

"Love all God's creation," says Fyodor Dostoyevski, "both the whole and every grain of sand. Love every leaf, every ray of light. Love the animals, love the plants, love each separate thing. If you love each thing you will pierce the mystery of God in all, and when you perceive this, you will from then on grow every day to a fuller understanding of it, until you come at last to love the whole world with a love that will then be all-embracing and eternal."

God Speaks in Many Ways

Writing in *America* for April 29, 1989, Father William J. O'Malley, S.J., said, "There is a natural potential in every human person that responds to the numinous and sacred in nature and art, and, if grace builds on nature, we can begin our movement toward the spirituality that deals with God by sensitizing children early to that more accessible and less intimidating union with the powerful and invisible forces all around them (that are, in fact, the aliveness of God).

"Take them to the woods and to the beach, away from buildings and billboards, Saturday cartoons, Trivial Pursuit and Monopoly. Ask if they can feel a presence there, something beyond the sigh of the wind and the harrumph of the waves."

According to Father William McNamara, a Carmelite monk and spiritual writer, virtually any human experience — seeing a good movie, talking to a close friend, holding hands with a loved one in front of a fire — can become an occasion for prayerful reflection. To become aware of God, says St. Thomas Aquinas, you must know his creation; but unless you surround yourself with those things and people and ideas that challenge you or move you or startle you, you will never be jolted into the radical amazement that engenders an awareness of God.

A young boy once told his mother, "Sometimes at church, I forget to pray. I just sit there, maybe thinking about how come the robins always know just when to come back in the spring."

"But, David," his mother said, "that is prayer. Wondering is a form of prayer. Some people call it

21

meditation. No matter what it's called, it all comes out to admitting that God is the greatest. Who else but God could engineer such a world and direct the flight of the birds?"

An Awareness of Mystery

Writing in *Notre Dame Magazine* for the summer of 1988, Edward Fisher reminded his readers, "We tend to think that knowledge solves mysteries, but for the educated it only brings more mysteries to the surface.

"The awe that comes with an awareness of mystery helps develop a religious spirit. Telescopes and microscopes can do wonders for your humility if they help you stand in awe of creation, realizing that when you open one door there are ten doors behind it — and behind each of those, ten more.

"God is not confined to theology; the Creator can be found in mathematics, history, and in all aspects of life."

In his book *St. Francis, Nature Mystic*, Edward A. Armstrong writes, "St. Francis was not only a mystic, but a nature mystic. Like Clement of Alexandria before him, he saw nature sanctified by the Incarnation; and like William Blake later, he could see heaven in a wildflower."

Dr. Frederick Franck is an artist of international stature and the author of more than twenty-five books. He holds doctorates in medicine, dentistry, and fine arts. According to Dr. Franck, "There is a great difference between 'looking at' and 'seeing.' My cat 'looks at' and pounces. Human beings have the capacity to see and identify with what they see. When I am actually fulfilled with something you could call awe, that is what you could call the manifestation of the divine."

It was in this spirit, no doubt, that the poet Lucille Crumley wrote:

Spring is:
God walking the earth
Through valleys, o'er hills,
Opening buds on bare branches,
Coloring daffodils.

2

What Do I Love When I Love You, My God?

The first time I saw God pictured on the silver screen was in the motion picture *Oh, God!* To tell the truth, God did not make even a cameo appearance in the film. George Burns was his stand-in. And Burns went on to assure the audience that he doesn't look or sound like God. The basic theme of the film was delightful: There is a God with whom we share the universe, and he cares about us.

As I was leaving the Metro theater in Prairie du Chien, Wisconsin, along with other moviegoers, a young boy remarked, "I wonder what God really looks like?"

Although the youngster did not know it, his question echoed that asked centuries ago by St. Augustine:

But what is it that I love when I love You, my God?

Not the beauty of any bodily thing, nor the order of the seasons, nor the brightness of the light that rejoices the eye, nor the sweet melodies of all songs, nor the sweet fragrance of flowers and ointments and spices; nor bread nor honey. None of these things do I love in loving my God. Yet, in a sense, I do love light, and melody, and fragrance and food and embrace when I love my God.

"And what is this God?" I asked the earth and it

answered: "I am not He." And all things that are in the earth made the same confession. I asked the sea and the deep and the creeping things, and they answered: "We are not your God; seek higher."

I asked the winds that blow, and the whole air with all that is in it answered: "I am not God!" I asked the heavens, the sun, the moon, the stars, and they answered: "Neither are we God whom you seek."

And I said to all the things that throng about the gateways of the senses: "Tell me of my God, since you are not He. Tell me something of Him."

And they cried out in a great voice: "He made us."

My question was my gazing upon them, and their beauty was the answer.

'Wherever I Go, You Are With Me'

"In You, God, my roots are fed," says Father Ignacio Larranaga, O.F.M. "I wrap myself in your arms. You are with me. With the palm of your right hand You cover my head. With the light of your eyes You penetrate my depths. I am a child who is cold and You warm me with your breath. You know perfectly well when I am at rest and when I begin to walk. My wanderings and path are more familiar to You than they are to me. I almost cannot believe it, but wherever I go, You are with me."

Father Ted Guzie, S.J., reminds us that "God is not 'up there' but He is 'right here.'"

God is someone humans encounter. There is no telling where each person may find the divine. Sacred moments are not always found in sacred places or sacred actions. The sacred moments will be found where they simply happen. No one can make them happen. They are gifts. But they might happen more often if people knew something about where and how to look.

Booker T. Washington told this story. There was a ship lost at sea for days. The crew had no drinking water and feared that they might die of thirst. At last they sighted a ship and as the two ships came closer they shouted: "Water, water everywhere but not a drop to drink. We are dying of thirst." The answer came back, "Drop down your buckets where you are." They did, and up came clear, fresh water. They had drifted into the mouth of the Amazon. God is to be found wherever people are.

The sacred moment may be a conversation with a friend, the touch of someone who cares.

The search for God runs like a fragile thread through our lives. On an expedition in China and Mongolia, Father Pierre Teilhard de Chardin offered Mass for a group of scientists, none of whom was Catholic. In his homily he said: "For each of us God, no doubt, hasn't the same precise meaning, the same face. Yet we beg His all-powerful Presence to crown our enterprise with success, and that any suffering which may befall us may be transferred in the higher joy of taking our little place in the universe and having done what was our duty."

When he was approaching fifty, Leo Tolstoy, one of the greatest writers in the history of literature, felt an emptiness within him. He was famous, wealthy, titled, happily married, and a proud father, yet he said: "Why wish for anything, or do anything? Is there any meaning in life?"

This profound melancholy lasted for about three years, but the answer Tolstoy found to his question changed his life. He discovered "those clear simple truths common to all men . . . the Spirit of God lives in man and the practical rule . . . that man should act toward others as he wishes others to act toward himself . . . God is a Spirit whose image lives in us."

Tolstoy renounced his title and began his work to relieve the oppressed. He wrote, "My prayer is like this: 'Who so abideth in love abideth in God, and God in him.

27

If we love one another His love is fulfilled in us. Brethren, let us love one another, for God is love."

On the eve of his ordination Emil Denemark expressed his views on what the priesthood meant to him: "I am convinced that every person, Christian or non-Christian, whether he or she is conscious of it or not, has a need and desire for God. All people want to hear about God; all desire somehow at least to taste him, to peek into heaven while still on earth. Life in modern society, unfortunately, has largely dulled these innate longings. The community of the Church, then, must have priests to nurture our conscious desires for God, and, furthermore, to uncover and spark those desires that remain silent, yet no less real and persistent.

To Know God as He Knows Us

"I am often awed by this aspect of the priesthood. For who can adequately speak of God to anyone? My consolation is that no one is expected to have a total vision of God; parts will always remain clouded until some epiphany in the future. The call of a priest is to verbalize for others what God in his various ways shows himself to be. I am acutely aware of the magnitude of my task, yet delighted at the opportunity to serve the profound reality of God's desire to have us know him as he knows us."

Father Karl Rahner, S.J., said: "We never know God directly, by some kind of intuition, as an object alongside other objects. We only know him as the distant horizon within which all our concrete acts of knowing and willing take place. It is the openness, the transcendence, at the core of our being that alone accounts for what is distinctively human in all our actions.

"Religion is not an arbitrary adjunct of our life; it is in the most strict sense what it is all about. It is the dimension that is implicit in and gives meaning to everything else, whether we are conscious of it or not. To be human is to be situated, initially in an unreflected way but nonetheless truly, before the reality of God. The dynamism that carries us along in the search for the good — the true — is a reaching for the infinite that is only possible because it is already rooted in the same God as the ground of being."

God Speaks to Us

Ladislaus Boros would have us keep in mind that the process by which we become conscious of God and his dealings with us is very mysterious. It can be likened to the formation of a stalactite or stalagmite, for it consists of thousands and thousands of little drops. It is not likely that we have ever grasped God as if he were the conclusion to an abstract train of thought. More probably, we think of him as the central point of countless allusions, connections, and relationships at the heart of our faithfulness, longing, and love.

We all have our own favorite image of God. For some of us God is the one who enlightens and warms everything. Many saints have experienced God's presence in this image of light. Great theologians have pointed to light as the sign of God's activity.

Mel Ellis tells us that many years ago he was attending an Easter sunrise service in a gigantic, natural amphitheater. At the moment the sun put its shining white crest above the horizon, the public-address system broke down and the minister's voice was silenced. As one, that throng of worshipers raised their eyes to the sky, and it was the holiest moment.

No wonder that William Ward wrote: "Every sunrise is a message from God and every sunset His signature."

Erich Przywara has written eloquently about God's presence in the world: "What is the deeper meaning of this ecstasy of spring? Is it not a premonition, pointing the way to a more perfect, eternal spring . . . to God, who, as Augustine said, is younger than everything that is young and newer than everything that is new? God is eternal spring."

One of the most outstanding scientists of this century was the late Charles A. Coulson, who said, "Science is helping to put a face on God. Science is one of the greatest praises of God, the understanding of what God has made."

I agree one hundred percent with the scientists who say, "Every new discovery in science is a further revelation of God."

"Rightly considered," says J. Elliott Ross, "modern scientific development gives us a profound conception of God because it gives us a better idea than heretofore of the inexhaustible activity of God."

In the Garden You Are Closer to God

In April 1976 Richard J. Daley, mayor of Chicago, boss of bosses, and presidential kingmaker, whispered into the microphone while the hushed audience strained to hear his every word. And the word was not about the economy or Democrats or Republicans; neither was it about governors or presidents.

Daley was talking about flowers. He was talking about how wonderful it was to explain to his grandchildren how a flower grows. "The greatest thing you can do," he said, "is to get close to the soil. When you're in the garden, you're closer to God than anywhere you can be in the world."

In New York City there is a memorial to John D. Rockefeller, Jr., founder of New York's Rockefeller Center. Inscribed on the green marble slab in the Center's Channel Gardens is the creed by which he lived: "I believe in the all-wise and all-loving God, named by whatever name; and that the individual's highest fulfillment, greatest happiness and widest usefulness are to be found in living in harmony with His will."

For the person who searches for God everywhere, the whole world becomes a challenge. Everywhere he turns, in everything he touches, he may discover something about God.

What Does God Look Like?

Seven-year-old Peggy was seated at the kitchen table with a tablet and set of crayons. Her mother looked up from her ironing board across the kitchen and asked, "What are you drawing, dear?"

"I'm drawing a picture of God," replied Peggy, her bright eyes sparkling like new dimes.

"But," objected Peggy's mother, "no one knows what God looks like."

With the unruffled confidence of youth, Peggy replied simply, "Now they will."

During January of 1979 I took the place of the pastor, Father Ed Thome, at St. John's Parish in Prairie du Chien, Wisconsin. During this time I taught religion to the grade-school students. One day I asked the students to express their ideas of God.

Armed with their imaginations they paged through magazines and newspapers in search of advertising slogans and names of products they could use in reference to God. Their results were posted on the school bulletin board. I'm delighted to be able to share these "insights" with you:

God is like General Electric — He lights your path.
God is like Coke — He's the real thing.
God is like Pan Am — He makes the going great.
God is like Sprite — You never get tired of him.
God is like Bayer Aspirin — He works wonders.
God is like Mercury — He has better ideas.
God is like Alka-Seltzer — Try him, you'll like him.
God is like Stokely Van Camp — He's the finest.
God is like Sears — He has everything.

God is like Lipton Tea Mix — He's cool!

God is like Fabergé — You won't have any doubts about him.

God is like Sanka Freeze-Dried — He's the one you like best.

God is like Invisible Scotch Tape — You can't see him, but you know he's there.

Sister Adele Rowland is a pioneer in the artistry of "haiku photography" — a montage technique that involves superimposing one image on another to communicate joyful aspects of life.

"I strive to alert people to the beauty and the excitement in the world," says Sister Adele. "I am endeavoring to alert viewers to an awareness of God in the world."

An art critic for the Los Angeles *Herald-Examiner* says of Sister Adele that she "simply awakens through her inventive images reflection of the presence of God."

In New York City on Christmas night of 1965, Duke Ellington and his orchestra praised the Lord with a concert of sacred music in the sanctuary of the Fifth Avenue Presbyterian Church. In front of the golden oak pews with their burgundy seat pads, in front of the stained-glass windows, they praised the Lord. On a bass viol John Lamb did what the psalmist said: "Praise him with stringed instruments."

Nobody took the psalmist more at his word than did Louis Bellson, who in six minutes of percussion solo, praised him upon "the loud cymbals."

There was honest communication when Cat Anderson praised the Lord in the way he knew best: on the trumpet. First, one solitary, cautious staccato, then a vibrant, pulsing clamor that erupted into a concerto of strident insistence. The trumpet seemed to pick up steam, as if driven by the ferocious intensity of the man at the mouthpiece. Faster and faster his fingers flew as he played his way far out on some experimental excursion all his own, as though he were exploring the outer reaches of some private dream world. Then suddenly, as if to shatter the mood, he abruptly broke off the elaborate — and all but indecipherable — musical pattern he had been weaving by running up and down the scales with a series of jubilant blasts.

"Every man," said Duke Ellington, "worships in his own language, and I know that there is no language God does not understand."

Each person has his or her own way of worshiping God. Lois Theuring tells us of her approach to God: "When I get up here on the mountaintop, where I can see for miles and miles around, I get all tongue-tied in my mind and all I can think of to say is, 'Wow, God, You're the greatest!' "

My Mother

My mother's special gift to her children was a sense of vivid delight in everything. Mother taught us children to stretch our hands out and take the world's wide gift of joy and beauty, to open wide our minds down to their inmost depths.

Although our life was frugal, we had the glowing vitality of Mother. Her energy rivaled that of the morning sun that came leaping through our kitchen window like a trumpet of dawn.

Mother took at face value the inspiring words of St. Irenaeus: "The glory of God is a person who is fully alive."

Mother believed that the beauty of the world and the beauty of every person reflects the beauty of God. The more we see of beauty, the closer we will be to God.

Mother accepted the beautiful truth that love is the ultimate human value, and the human is permeated with the divine. Our point of contact with the divine is the human, and to embrace the one is to embrace the other. In the words of St. John, "He who abides in love abides in God and God in him."

We see God in the face of a sleeping babe, in the bright-eyed wonderment of children at Christmas, in the eyes of lovers as they walk hand-in-hand. We see God in the older person, in the hands gnarled and bent from a life of work.

The gift of friendship is the nicest gift of all. It comes wrapped in warmth and understanding, and tied with love.

If you search the world around, this thing above all you will find. Of all the gifts from God above, the greatest gift to man is love.

No wonder that Helen Steiner Rice wrote:

I've never seen God,
but I know how I feel —
It's people like you
who make Him "So Real" —
My God is no stranger,
He's friendly and gay,
And He doesn't ask me to weep when I pray —
It seems that I pass Him
so often each day
In the faces of people I meet on my way —
He's in the stars in the heavens,
a smile on some face,
A leaf on a tree or a rose in a vase —
He's winter and autumn
and summer and spring,
In short, God Is Every Real, Wonderful Thing —
I wish I might meet Him
much more than I do,
I would if there were
More People Like You.

No wonder that Walt Whitman said, "I see something of God each hour of the twenty-four, and each moment then, in the faces of men and women I see God, and in my own face in the glass."

The story is told of a little boy with his grandfather on the banks of a river. Their conversation covered everything from where fish go at night to why the sun is so red on the horizon. In the stillness and beauty that come in summer twilight, the boy asked, "Gramps, can anyone see God?"

"Son," his grandfather answered, "it's getting so I can't see anything but God."

"Every morning," said James Russell Lowell, "lean thine arms awhile upon the window-sill of heaven, and gaze upon the Lord. Then, with that vision in thy heart, turn strong to meet the day."

Galileo, in speaking of God, tells us: "The sun, with all its planets moving around it, can ripen the smallest bunch of grapes as if it had nothing else to do. Why then should I doubt His power?"

According to Rollo May, the power of beauty is its capacity to put us in touch with God. "When we see something beautiful we tend to be silent, and out of this silence comes a feeling of ecstacy and of eternity, of something that lasts forever. This is an experience of the power of beauty. It is an experience which can have a profound effect on our lives if we so allow it."

In the Sunday bulletin for St. Cecilia's Cathedral in Omaha, Nebraska, for January 22, 1989, the pastor, Father Vincent P. Mainelli, wrote: "In beauty, especially the beauty of creation, we can find God. St. Francis is one of the most celebrated preachers of this truth, especially in his 'Canticle to the Sun,' and in his love for all creatures in whom he saw God. And the pages of the Bible, especially the Psalms, often break forth with the praise of God reflected in the majesty of the mountains, the beauty of the stars, the brightness of the sun. Cathedrals in their beauty are meant to call us to rejoice in the beauty of God."

3

The Many Faces of God

Some months ago I came across an article in *Liguorian* magazine entitled "The Many Faces of God." I was so delighted with this article I wrote to the author, Sister Rose Michael Weber, S.C., for permission to reprint it. Thanks to her courtesy and kindness, I can share her outlook with you.

"Right after God created the angels, she made the librarians." These words by Franklyn Peterson jumped off the pages of a professional journal and made me laugh outright. As a plenty-year-old Sister of Charity, I can hardly be accused of being a feminist, but sometimes a quip or a cartoon forces me to think when a scholarly article doesn't.

I asked myself, How do I view God? As a father, a mother, a friend? Yes, to all three — and sometimes as a child, to boot.

I see God within me and around me as many different personalities — all of them valid.

I see God as a father when I need a protector, when I'm walking home from Mass on a dark night and hear a sound in the bushes. "O God, my Father, take care of me," I pray and huddle close to him as I once huddled close to my own father when I was afraid.

I see God as a father when I am in trouble through my own fault. As a child, when my family had just moved, I set about exploring all the possibilities of our new house and grounds. I intrepidly climbed from the ashpit onto the tool shed. Then, with quite a strain, I climbed onto the roof of the garage. I was queen of all I surveyed and enjoyed this lofty position for quite a while. When my father called me to lunch, I yelled triumphantly, "Look where I am!"

"That's fine," he answered, "but how are you going to get down safely?" That last word really got me. Just HOW was I going to get back to earth without falling? I was really scared. He directed me step-by-step until I could jump into the strong, loving protection of his arms.

I see God as a father when I need courage to try something new. The biggest step in my teenage life was leaving home for college thirteen hundred miles away. The last night at home I was fighting tears, premature homesickness, and just plain panic. My father came, put his arms around me, shook my shoulders, and reminded me that, since I had received a scholarship, this was really God's gift to me. He assured me that I would meet new friends. He was right. This year I met with my companions of those early years to celebrate the golden jubilee of our college graduation.

I see God as a mother when I need tenderness. When I am in pain or hurting from rejection, I pray for those qualities I remember in my mother. My work in a retreat center can be quite chaotic and I often wonder where I can find the peace and serenity we provide for others. God as mother encourages me to take a quiet moment, attune myself to peace and joy, and soon I too share in divine serenity.

I see God as my mother when I need to be told I'm lovable just the way I am. My own mother did that beautifully when I was not chosen to crown the Blessed Mother in the eighth grade. I was devastated because the girl selected was tall, beautiful, bright, and full of confidence. Mamma wiped away my tears, brushed back my hair, and told me that no one could ever be as lovely

38

as her little daughter, that I pleased her and the Blessed Mother with everything from my good grades to seeing beauty in flowers, people, and funny situations. "The May Crowning will only last for one hour. You will last forever as my lovable little girl."

I see God as my mother when I need a peacemaker in my life. When I have disagreed with or offended someone else, I go to God just as I would to my own mother. Once a family friend whom I loved hurt me with a remark about something I was wearing. I was in tears. My mother healed the pain with her forgiving, tolerant words. "It was a mistake of the head and not the heart." Wasn't that a Godlike response? It was easy to again show love to my favorite neighbor.

I see God as a mother when I view life-giving nature, not just in the birth of a baby but in the rebirth of spring after a hard, cold winter. Like a mother's love, God warms the earth, and lilies bloom to tell of the Resurrection; ice-bound streams melt and flow, teaching hearts and hands to reach out to others.

I see God as a mother when I experience loss — loss of a friend through moving or death, loss of a job, loss of energy, or loss of things. Mothers are great consolers. When I was a child, we lost our house through a mortgage foreclosure. That home was my mother's dream-come-true. I thought she would be crushed. Little did I know of her faith and courage. With my arms around her, I said I wished I was a grown-up with lots of money so I could pay off the mortgage. Her consoling words taught me a major lesson. "Let's thank God we had the house when you children were little."

Sometimes I see God as a friend. When I need someone to listen but not necessarily to advise. There is Chris, before whom I can be truly my fractured, repellent, or motor-mouthed self. With her I can laugh, cry, joke, argue, suggest, refuse — and she will listen. She doesn't give advice, yet her few loving words indicate God's direction. God is truly my friend through her.

I see God as a friend in whom I can confide dreams, feelings, and fears because he really knows me, is interested in how I feel, what and when I love. He can do more than a flesh-and-blood friend. He can fulfill these dreams, dissipate these fears, and change, enlarge, or present these feelings to my consciousness in such a way as to make me new.

I see God as a friend who doesn't criticize me for being the way I am but loves me into becoming a better person. Like the Sister who urges me to see "the whole picture" of religious life, the beauty in its diversity and change, and not to concentrate on the corner of pain or the crack through which loved and loving people have left.

I see God as a friend when I'm lonely and he draws me to the chapel. There I am no longer alone. His presence is almost like the touch of a hand. Or, on a warm autumn day, loneliness may direct me to see God outdoors, where he waves friendly greeting in the dancing leaves, smiles with sunlit waters, speaks his message on the wind through the pines — and I return calmed, encouraged, and definitely not alone.

Finally, I sometimes see God as a child, especially as I watch his playful work and humor operating in life around me. When he sends rain during the outdoor liturgy at the family retreat with sixty-seven children, I know he's not that concerned about the solemnity of our meal with him.

When he leads me to don a Halloween costume, wear a plastic bucket for a mask, and appear with another Sister with a banner declaring we are "Buckets of Fun," I know he is telling me it's okay to play, to laugh, and to enjoy life.

Another article that fascinated me appeared in *Maryknoll* magazine. It was entitled "The Feminine

Face of God." The author is Dr. Kathleen M. O'Connor, assistant professor of biblical studies at Maryknoll School of Theology. Thanks to her kindness and generosity I can also share her insights with you.

Human language about God is like sunlight in a dark forest. It pierces the thickness to light one tree with gold, and leaves the remainder in mysterious shadow. Human language provides us with only a glimpse of divinity, even if the images come from the graced insights of prophets.

"Can a mother forget her child? Yet even if your mother should forget you, I will not forget you, says Yahweh. See I have carved you in the palm of my hand." Through this rich and powerful image of motherhood, the Prophet Isaiah (49:15-16) portrays God's fidelity as so utterly staunch and loving that it surpasses a human mother's faithfulness.

Profound as the experience of motherhood may be, however, it is still too limited to describe what God is like because divinity eludes every attempt to be captured by human language or human experience. The Bible is firm on this point. God is always more than we can imagine or express. The Bible shows that every time God's people thought they understood God or how God behaves, something happened to shatter that security. The light shifted to another quality of God's love.

When Israel, for instance, settled in the Promised Land, the people believed that God lived there in the Temple especially close to them. But when the foreign nation of Babylon conquered their homeland, God seemed to disappear from their midst. The Israelites had to learn that God was not restricted to the land or to the Temple. God went with them to that alien place where they were prisoners of war and lived among them.

41

And when Jesus came, the people's expectations of God were again exploded. They did not expect God to act through a Messiah who dined with whores and tax collectors collaborating with the occupying Roman authorities. Nor had they anticipated that God would be revealed through the death of a condemned criminal.

In our time, light is shifting to another aspect of God which has long been in darkness. God has a feminine side. God is not a man but God who transcends all human notions, even that of sexuality. To speak of God only as a male person is to make God small.

God is not only our Father; God is also our Mother who loves us beyond measure (Isaiah 49:15-16).

God is not only the shepherd who leaves the 99 to find the one lost sheep; God is also the peasant woman who sweeps her house clean until she finds the one lost coin, just as so many poor women have always done (Luke 15:3-10).

God is the man who plants and waters the mustard seed in his garden until this smallest of seeds grows into a huge tree; God is also the woman who folds a little bit of yeast into a bowl of flour until the dough rises and marvelously doubles itself (Luke 13:18-21).

That is the way Jesus taught the people about God. God is like men in everyday experience and God is like women in that same arena of everyday life.

In the Old Testament, God is described as the nurturing parent who lifts the helpless child to her cheek and who teaches it to walk (Hosea 11:1-4). The quality of mercy which is used so often about God in the Old Testament comes from the Hebrew word which means womb. God's compassionate mercy is like the feelings of bondedness, pride and pity that a mother has for the babe in her womb. Though God is beyond all our ideas, beyond masculinity and femininity, God can be described appropriately as feminine, the Mother of us all who gives us birth and nurtures us to our full humanity.

But why is it important to think and speak about God in feminine terms?

First of all, it reminds us that God's ways are not our ways. To reduce God too strictly to any mode of human experience is to worship an idol, to make God according to our image, to forget that we are creatures.

When we think about God as feminine, we expand our notions of what God might be like. We add to our society's one-sided view of masculinity — strength, power and justice — the other "feminine" side of human existence — compassion, gentleness and warmth. Though these are too limited views of the characteristics of either sex, the fact that our society holds them and names God with only masculine images indicates that our understanding of God is also one-sided.

Another important reason to recognize the feminine in God is that always thinking of God as masculine indirectly teaches us that men make a better image or representative of God than women. But in the first creation story in the Book of Genesis God said, "Let us make humanity in our image, after our likeness. . . . So God created humanity, male and female."

Thus, to have a glimpse of God, to take advantage of the sunlight in the forest, we must look at both male and female. Together men and women image God mutually and co-responsibly. This means that women can teach us as much about God as men. It means that women and men are equal in dignity and authority, for God gave to both the command, "Fill the earth and subdue it and have dominion over the fish and the birds and over every living thing."

Because in the past most of us thought of God as a male being, it somehow followed that men always should be in charge — in government, in the Church, in business and in the family. Today society is challenging this partial view. Listening to this questioning with open hearts will help us get another glimpse of the mysterious otherness of God.

The God of Love

Father Peter G. van Breemen, S.J., would have us keep in mind the following: "If it is true that to a certain extent we make our images of God, it is no less true and probably more important what our images of God make us. Eventually we become like the God we image. The belief in God as Abba [Father] nurtures confident, free persons. The God of love, as in John's first letter, fosters a loving people."

Ladislaus Boros, a spiritual writer, informs us, "Each of us has her own favorite image of God. For many of us it is light. We see God as the one who enlightens and warms everything. Many saints have experienced God's presence in this image of light, and great theologians have pointed to light as the sign of God's activity in the world."

Who is God? St. John says God is love. Love is his nature. God does not have love; he is love.

Francine M. O'Connor wrote this delightful poem about a little girl's perception of God:

That night when Amy went to her room,
she thought about God with all her might.
Suddenly she sat up straight in her bed,
for she knew exactly what God must be like.

"He's as loving as Mom and as brave as Dad.
He's as kind and helpful as brother Tim.
He teaches me like my teacher in school —
Oh, yes, now I think I really know him!"

My mother's favorite flower was the rose. Her garden overflowed with them. Mother agreed wholeheartedly with the poet Tabitha Ritzmann:

A rose — what a regal fragrant flower —
Unfolding silently its loveliness!
I look into its depth of beauty
And know it is God's gift, to cheer and bless.

No human could ever fashion
One velvet petal or leaf of green.
With reverence I behold this wonder
And feel the nearness of a Love unseen!

One of the most popular Catholic authors in the world today is the Jesuit Father John Powell. His books have sold over eleven million copies. Father Powell views his writing and media work as a means to help people believe in themselves, to recognize their goodness and giftedness, and to see themselves as children of a loving God.

In his delightful book *He Touched Me*, Father Powell reminds us that "the soul which has been touched by God will be deepened in his awareness of the world around him. He will see with his new eyes the beauty of the world; he will hear its music and poetry and know that it is a beautiful world.

"He will also find himself in deeper contact with the sadness in the hearts of men. He will notice a new awareness, a new aliveness. As old St. Irenaeus, in the second century, once said: 'The glory of God is a man fully alive.' The true touch of God results in a new and vital 'Yes' to life."

Since I wished my students to have this life-giving, energizing vision of the universe mentioned by Father Powell, I began each of my science classes, during the thirty years I taught at Campion High School, Prairie du Chien, Wisconsin, with Psalm 19: "The heavens show forth the glory of God, and the sky declares the work of his hands."

In his instructive and inspiring book *Fully Human,*

Fully Alive, Father Powell says, "Blessed are the children who receive a life-giving, energizing vision of the universe. They will be taught to wonder, to be filled with curiosity, to admire. Their leisure will be filled with nature walks, stargazing, planting gardens, bird-watching, and rock- or seashell-collecting. They will learn to care for their own pets, to distinguish species of flowers and trees as well as cloud formations.

"Children learn to cherish life as a beautiful opportunity or to despise it as a drudgery. They discover that the world is wide and warm and beautiful, or they walk along with eyes cast down through an unexamined world. It is all a matter of the vision they inherit. This vision is certainly the most important legacy of a child's parents and first teachers."

Laughter, Hope, and Goodness

At a symposium on religion held at Creighton University in Omaha, Nebraska, in October of 1986, the speakers brought home the fact that Christianity stands for what life is at its best: laughter, hope, and the goodness of the world. The Christian imagination sees God everywhere and disclosing himself through all things. The many gifts we receive from God reassure us that we are enveloped in an atmosphere of graciousness, hope, and love.

If we open the windows of our minds and look out upon the wonder-filled universe all about us, we will become aware of our wonderful God. We will come to realize how God is giving us his gifts on every side. We will discover that God is working for us in many, many magnificent ways.

4

Troubadours of God

I'm always delighted and thrilled to discover how different people approach God, and how they proclaim his name.

A most extraordinary person, Sister Thea Bowman, a black nun, who was the granddaughter of a slave, died on March 30, 1990. It was through music that Sister Thea came to God, and it was through music that she led others to God.

Six days before her death, Sister Thea was named the 1990 recipient of the prestigious Laetare Medal from Notre Dame University, the highest honor given to American Catholics.

Sister Thea helped to found — and served on — the faculty of the Institute of Black Catholic Studies at Xavier University in New Orleans, the only black Catholic university in the Western hemisphere. She helped organize the 1987 Black Catholic Congress. She was the director of Intercultural Awareness for the Diocese of Jackson. She is credited with having incorporated African rituals and dances, as well as African-American folk songs into the Mass.

"We do not want to change the theology of the Church," she explained to those made uneasy by any deviation from white, European liturgical expression. "We just want to express theology within the roots of our black spiritual culture."

At her funeral Mass on April 3, 1990, Cardinal Bernard F. Law of Boston proclaimed her the true balm of

Gilead: "Sister Thea possessed the charismatic gifts to heal, to bring joy to the Church. She was a poet, preacher, master-teacher and blessed with an extraordinary voice. She challenged us to own our individuality, yet pleaded for us to be one in Christ. This was her song."

The Most Rev. John H. Ricard, S.S.J., auxiliary bishop of Baltimore, called Sister Thea the "springtime in everyone's life" and noted how appropriate that she die in the spring: "how fitting that we celebrate the new life of Sister Thea in this the spring."

'Sashaying Into Our Lives'

Sister Francesca Thompson, Franciscan nun and assistant dean of Fordham University, Bronx, New York, said of Sister Thea, "She was the God-gilded voice sent dancing, swaying, sashaying into our lives. She was song. She was the joyous Franciscan always."

Father Bede Abram, celebrant of the Mass, prayed in conclusion: "O God, as you did not lose her in her coming to us, we do not lose her in her going back to you."

Sister Thea will live on in the lives of all she touched.

One of my previous students, Jack Horkheimer, is the director of Florida's Miami Space Transit Planetarium. He is also a writer and producer of TV specials. He is the host of his own nightly TV series known as *Star Hustler*. For the international premiere of his multimedia special, *Starbound*, Jack wrote this prologue:

Once upon a time. . .
In a galaxy not so very far away. . .
There existed a creature strange,
With an insatiable thirst for knowledge.
Now this is the *peculiar* part:
The more it learned, the less it knew. . .
For with every answer, came another question.

Now this is the beautiful part:
Of all the creature's thirsts,
This one . . . brought him closest . . . to the Gods.

Jack Horkheimer was born in rural Wisconsin in 1938. As a young boy he was awed by the beauty of the star-filled winter skies. Horkheimer went to under-graduate and graduate school at Purdue University in Indiana. Before he left Indiana, something special happened to him.

"I was in my room looking out a window at a clear moonless night," he explains. "In the background, I heard a rabbi on the TV saying, 'There is only one kind of prayer: when you look at something and are stunned by its beauty, and when you are stunned by the complexity and genius behind it, that is prayer, because that is praise and wonder and awe.' I was looking at the stars, and suddenly I saw them as giant globes sprinkled through space. I was stunned by the universe."

First Mass in the Air

During the mid-thirties, when I was a student at St. Louis University, I had the golden opportunity of meeting Father Paul Schulte, O.M.I. He was known as "The Flying Priest."

Father Schulte holds the honor of saying the first Mass in the air. The date was May 8, 1936. The *Hindenburg*, the ill-fated dirigible (which crashed on May 6, 1937), was on its sixty-two-hour maiden voyage from Germany to Lakehurst, New Jersey.

In his address during the Mass, Father Schulte said, "Glory to God the Father, who created the earth; and to God the Son, who redeemed the earth; and to God the Holy Spirit who hallowed the earth. Let the 'Amen' be pronounced by the skies and the marvelous clouds which surround us, by the ocean over which we are hovering, by the sun, the breeze, and the stars. Let the 'Amen' be spoken by the motors, the wonderful airship, the crew, the passengers. Glory be to Thee today, tomorrow, and in all eternity. Amen."

Father Schulte concluded the Mass by dedicating the wide realm of the air to Christ, the King.

'Operation Highjump'

In the mid-1950s I was riding the Burlington *Twin Cities Zephyr* from St. Paul to Chicago. By pure good luck I found myself sitting with Father William J. Menster, the chaplain for Richard E. Byrd's Antarctic expedition "Operation Highjump" in 1947.

Father Menster informed me that from the moment the expedition left the States, he was conscious of his own peculiar position on this fourth Antarctic expedition. He was to be the first priest ever to enter the Antarctic Circle.

"During the course of our trip south," said Father Menster, "I had spoken often with Admiral Cruzen about the blessing of Antarctica.

"Originally I had planned an outdoor general service and Mass, but I had not anticipated the bitter cold of the Ross Ice Shelf, the knifing winds that made unnecessary exposure a foolish risk. The mess tent was large enough to hold all the men for the services, so I decided on the afternoon of January 26, 1947, for the first Antarctic Mass."

During the homily Father Menster read the following prayer which he had composed for the blessing of the continent: "O Almighty and Eternal God, Maker of heaven and earth and all things, from Thy heavenly throne behold us, Thy servants here assembled to offer Thee for the first time from this great continent, public adoration, praise, and thanks.

"We are inspired by its vastness and whiteness to thoughts of our insignificance and unworthiness and of

52

Thy greatness. We humbly thank Thee for the privilege that is ours today, of blessing and consecrating it to Thy service."

In the preface he wrote to the book *Strong Men South*, Admiral Byrd said, "The whole Antarctic might be referred to as a mighty cathedral of glittering ice and painted sky erected by the Lord's own hand.

"Far from the turmoil of the world, it is the ideal retreat for those who would find a more intimate touch with the infinite Greatness and Goodness."

With Crooked Lines

The most enjoyable book I have read in many years is *With Crooked Lines*, written by my good friend Father James Hart McCown, S.J. It was published in 1990 by the Spring Hill College Press, Mobile, Alabama. I was so delighted with this book I wrote to Father McCown and secured permission to share the following with you these experiences from his boyhood.

Five of us McCowns slept year-round on our broad, screened-in upstairs front porch. One night I awoke to listen to the incredible soloing of a mockingbird under a full moon. I don't think the nightingale can surpass this common bird of the south when he is driven into a frenzy of joy by the full moon and the quickening surge of the mating season.

His song is loud, limpid, varied to an incredible degree; first soft, then trilling, then bursting into a brilliant crescendo. And all the time he sits on the tiptop of a tree in clear sight. And every few moments he flutters ten feet straight up into the air, then back down to his perch singing his heart out during the aerial dance. (Some killjoy ornithologists claim that this is only a territorial assertion. Don't listen to them. God is being sung to!)

This night I arose to listen, and was thrilled. And

ready for things divine. So, when I looked up and beheld four luminous arms of a cross extending out from the moon I became very happy. I was having a vision. I was undoubtedly a saint. I knew from holy pictures how ecstatic saints looked, and I knew how they acted from stories that Sister Clotilda read to us. I folded my hands and yearned up toward Heaven, feeling close to God.

Then I began to look around. Strange, but the street light on Dauphin Street had the same miraculous cross radiating from it. I grew wary. Then, when a late-night automobile came chugging down the street with both yellow headlights exuding luminous yellow crosses to God's glory, such as any light will do if viewed through a spread of metal mosquito netting, this young visionary of God climbed down humbly from his small Cloud Nine.

In his ninth summer young James McCown was invited to visit the Toomer family at Battles Wharf. This is how he recalls that episode: "A significant thing, the memory of which stayed with me all my life and undoubtedly shaped my life, happened in my stay with the Toomers. Mrs. Annie Toomer, my mother's best friend, was always the most beautiful woman in the world to me. She had olive skin and heavy brown hair that hung to her waist and blazed in the sun with an auburn radiance when she stood in the back yard to dry it after a swim. I loved to watch her.

"A neighbor boy, a little older than I, told me that he did not believe in God. It was just 'nature' that did all these clever things. His anti-theology, coming to me only a few years after Santa Claus had been demythologized, sounded good to me, sort of grown-up. So, I, too, began to profess atheism, to brag about my unbelief. Mrs. Annie heard me. She waited for the proper moment when she and I were alone to explain to me sweetly and convincingly, how nature is nothing more than God's power and direction of all the wonderful things around us, how God uses them to show us how much He loves us, and to give us a hint of how wonderful He is. Immediately I became a believer again, grateful forever to this understanding woman for her wise and timely guidance."

The above episode from the life of Father McCown reminds me that some time ago I received a letter from a grandmother in Florida. Mrs. Wildene Ickes wrote: "Yesterday I took my four-year-old granddaughter, Karissa, to the beach. I said to her, 'Isn't this a beautiful day? Look at the pelicans and sea gulls flying over the ocean. Look at the blue sky, the white clouds. Touch the warm water and the soft sand.'

"Karissa replied, 'It is beautiful.'

"Then I said, 'Karissa, God made all these things and He made us. Each day we should thank Him for everything because without Him we would be nothing.' "

Blaise Pascal was one of the great mathematicians and scientists in France during the seventeenth century. He is remembered as the discoverer of Pascal's law: The pressure exerted on a confined liquid is transmitted undiminished in all directions. Important applications of Pascal's law are the hydraulic brakes in your car and the automobile lift in service stations. Pascal also proved that air pressure decreases with altitude. He is credited with inventing the first calculator and the first system of public transportation in Europe.

Take the Risk of Loving God

Pascal found it exciting to be a believer in God. He felt that faith has to do with love — with choosing to love and give yourself to an invisible someone.

Pascal believed that if there is a risk in giving love to a God you cannot see, it is a risk well worth taking.

Most of the electricity we use today is generated by spinning coils of copper wire inside a magnetic field.

The scientist who showed us how to generate electricity with a magnet and a coil of wire is Michael Faraday. He was born on September 22, 1791, in Newington, a suburb of London. He died on August 25, 1867.

Faraday was honored by membership in many scientific societies. In 1863 he was elected a foreign member of the United States National Academy of Sciences.

Faraday looked upon the pursuit of science as essentially a search for God. "These," he once said of the physical laws, "are the glimmerings we have of the second causes by which the one Great Cause works His wonders and governs the earth.

"The book of nature, which we read is written by the finger of God. He has set His testimony (like a rainbow) in the heavens."

Faraday experienced genuine curiosity and real joy in his whole approach to nature. The contemplation of nature produced in Faraday a kind of spiritual exaltation. His religious feeling and philosophy could not be kept apart; there was a habitual overflow of the one into the other.

In a lecture in 1847 Faraday said, "Our philosophy, whilst it shows us these things, should lead us to think of Him who hath wrought them, 'for the invisible things of Him from the creation of the world are clearly seen being understood by the things that are made, even His eternal power and Godhead' (Romans 1:20)."

A colleague of Faraday, John Tyndall, said of Faraday, "What to him was the splendor of a palace compared with a thunderstorm upon Brighton Downs — what among all the applications of royalty to compare with the setting sun? I refer to a thunderstorm and a sunset because these things excited a kind of ecstasy in his mind."

These words of a poet — "The man who stands to watch a sunset, moves in close to God" — are only too true in respect to Michael Faraday. He took special delight and happiness in that hushed and breathless moment of the day when shadows creep out of the sides of the hills, and the forest is filled with mysterious colors that have no name. Clouds descend the stairway of the sky to mingle with the mountain peaks. From the copper canyons of the West they steal the glowing embers of the dying sun and scatter them in blazing climax to light campfires in the sky.

This is an hour of silence. An hour made for prayer. Perhaps here, indeed, is the secret of its enchantment, that all creation at this hour praises God, singing of his beauty, and entreating his benediction for the night. At this time the heart kneels, and did all men with one accord kneel too, the kingdom of God would without hindrance and without delay be established on earth.

'A Quest for Absolute Beauty'

One of the most outstanding books to cross my horizon during the years when I was a student at St. Louis University was *Man, The Unknown*. It was published in 1935 and became a nationwide best seller. It was called the "most discussed" book of the era. The author, Dr. Alexis Carrel, received the Nobel Prize for his success in suturing blood vessels and in the transplanting of organs. He has been called the most original physiological surgeon of the century. Dr. Carrel became a Catholic after witnessing miracles at Lourdes. He never quite recovered from his awe at seeing a large cancerous sore on a workman's hand shrivel to a scar before his eyes.

According to Dr. Carrel, "Religious activity consists of a vague aspiration toward a power transcending this world, a kind of unformulated prayer, a quest for absolute beauty. It is splendidly generous. It brings to man an inner strength, spiritual light, ineffable peace."

William Jennings Bryan was a lawyer and politician who made use of a watermelon seed to tell the story of

God's infinite power. Thanks to the kindness and courtesy of the *Omaha World-Herald* newspaper, I can give you Mr. Bryan's exact words:

> I was eating a piece of watermelon some months ago and was struck with its beauty. I took some of the seed and dried them and weighed them. Then I applied mathematics to the forty-pound melon.
>
> One of these seeds, put into the ground when warmed by the sun and moistened by the rain, goes to work; it gathers from somewhere two hundred thousand times its own weight and, forcing the raw material through a tiny stem, constructs a watermelon.
>
> It covers the outside with a coating of green; inside the green it puts a layer of white, and within the white a core of red, and all through the red it scatters seeds, each one capable of continuing the work of reproduction.
>
> Where did that seed get its tremendous power? Where did it find its coloring matter? How did it collect the flavoring extract? How did it build a watermelon?
>
> Everything that grows tells a like story of infinite power.

According to William Jennings Bryan, "Man is a religious being; the heart instinctively seeks for a God. Whether he worships on the banks of the Ganges, prays with his face upturned to the sun, kneels toward Mecca, or, regarding all space as a temple, communes with the Heavenly Father according to the Christian creed, man is essentially devout."

I was fascinated by what Bryan had to say about life after death.

> And immortality! Who will estimate the peace which a belief in a future life has brought to the sorrowing?
>
> To every created thing God has given a tongue that proclaims a resurrection.

If God deigns to touch with divine power the cold and pulseless heart of the buried acorn and to make it burst forth from its prison walls, will He leave neglected in the earth the soul of man, made in the image of his Creator?

If God stoops to give to the rose bush, whose withered blossoms float upon the autumn breeze, the sweet assurance of another springtime, will He refuse the words of hope to come?

If matter, mute and inanimate, though changed by the forces of nature into a multitude of forms, can never die, will the spirit of man suffer annihilation when it has paid a brief visit like a royal guest to this tenement of clay?

No, I am as sure that there is another life as I am that I live today!

In Cairo, Egypt, I secured a few grains of wheat that had slumbered for more than 3,000 years in an Egyptian tomb. As I looked at them this thought came into my mind: if one of those grains had been planted on the banks of the Nile the year after it grew, and all its lineal descendants planted and replanted from that time until now, its progeny would today be sufficiently numerous to feed the teeming millions of the world.

There is in the grain of wheat an invisible something which has power to discard the body that we see and from earth and air fashion a new body so much like the old one that we cannot tell the one from the other.

If this invisible germ of life in the grain of wheat can thus pass unimpaired through 3,000 resurrections, I shall not doubt that my soul has power to clothe itself with a body suited to its new existence when this earthly frame has crumbled into dust.

It is interesting to note that these truths stated by William Jennings Bryan were boldly emphasized by the world's greatest rocket expert, Dr. Wernher von Braun, the man responsible for putting our astronauts on the moon.

"Scientists now believe," said von Braun, "that in nature, matter cannot be destroyed without being converted into energy. Not even the tiniest particle can disappear without a trace. Nature does not know extinction — only transformation. Would God have less regard for His masterpiece of creation, the human soul?

"Immortality, to me, is the continuity of our spiritual existence after death. Since the dawn of history, man has believed in immortality."

Father Walter J. Burghardt, S.J., of Georgetown University is one of the outstanding theologians in the United States and has contributed articles to many magazines. In February 1983 Father Burghardt had a beautiful article in *Hospital Progress*. This article was reprinted in condensed form in *The Catholic Digest* in July of the same year.

Father Burghardt's comments on wonder are so fascinating that I wrote to him for permission to share his penetrating insights with you. Thanks to his courtesy and kindness, I can share the following with you:

> Several years before his death in 1972, Rabbi Heschel suffered a near-fatal heart attack from which he never fully recovered. A dear friend visiting him then found him woefully weak. Just about able to whisper, Heschel said to him: "Sam, when I regained consciousness, my first feeling was not of despair or anger. I felt only gratitude to God for my life, for every moment I had lived. I was ready to depart. 'Take me, O Lord,' I thought, 'I have seen so many miracles in my lifetime.'"
> Exhausted by the effort, Heschel paused, then added: "This is what I meant when I wrote (in the preface to his book of Yiddish poems): 'I did not ask for success; I asked for wonder. And You gave it to me.'
> "Essential to your apostolate, I submit, is a sense of

wonder. By 'wonder' I do not mean doubt or despair: I wonder if life is really worth living. I do not mean uncertainty: I wonder whether Israel should permit a Palestinian state.

"No, in the grasp of wonder I'm surprised. I'm amazed. I marvel, I'm delighted, I'm enraptured. I'm in awe. It's Moses before the burning bush, 'afraid to look at God' (Exod. 3:6), and Mary, newly God's mother: 'My spirit rejoices in God my Savior' (Lk. 1:47). It's Stephen about to be stoned: 'I see the Son of Man standing at the right hand of God' (Acts 7:56), and Michelangelo striking his sculptured Moses and commanding him: 'Speak!' It's Ignatius Loyola in ecstasy as he eyes the sky at night, Teresa of Ávila ravished by a rose. It's doubting Thomas discovering his God in the wounds of Jesus, Mother Teresa spying the face of Christ in the tortured poor. It's America thrilling to footsteps on the moon, a child casting his kite to the winds. It's mother looking with love on her newborn infant. It's the wonder of the first kiss.

"Such wonder must possess you because wonder is what marks a religious man, a religious woman. Because wonder — over and above faith — should be your reaction to the endless series of God's wonderful works, the story of a God who, as the Book of Job tells us, 'does great things and unsearchable, marvelous things, without number' (Job 9:10)."

Heschel concluded: "As civilization advances, the sense of wonder declines." This is not a tirade against technology. I am simply resonating to Heschel's alarm: "Mankind will not perish for want of information . . . only for want of appreciation." To appreciate not only the new but the old, not only the miracle that shatters nature but the wonder that is every day. When did I last marvel not at what I saw — the Rodin exhibit, *Star Wars*, the Boston Celtics or Los Angeles Lakers, Mother Teresa — but that I see, that with a flicker of eyelids I can span a small world? Must I grow deaf with Beethoven before I touch my ears with reverence? Does it amaze me that I can shape an idea, tell you how I feel, touch my fingers to another's face, to a flower?

The religious Jew thanks God three times a day for the wonder of being, for God's amazing blessings: "We thank Thee . . . for thy miracles which are daily with us, for thy continued marvels. . . ."

About to drink a glass of water, the Jew recalls the eternal mystery of creation: "Blessed be Thou . . . by whose word all things come into being."

This is not to blind ourselves to sin and war, to disease and death. These are terribly real. And still we have to see, with Gerard Manley Hopkins, that "the world is charged with the grandeur of God."

I have to live my ordinary day in the presence of the living God. Such, very simply, was Heschel's secret. For him the question of religion was what we do with the presence of God. Here He is, Paul told the Athenians, "not far from each one of us" (Acts 17:27). Here He is, in our gathering together and in our war-torn world, on our altar and on the face of this cancerous lump of clay. How do we live in the presence of the living God?

In wonder indeed, ceaselessly surprised by the trace of God all around us. But wonder need not paralyze us: wonder need not mean wide-eyed inactivity. Heschel proved that. Theologian and historian, poet and mystic, he moved from his study to social issues: Vietnam and poverty, civil rights and racism, Russian Jewry and Israel.

He had experienced Hitler's Germany, but because he was spared the flames that devoured his family and his community, he felt a special burden: to remind us that, despite the absurdity and apathy that surrounds us, "The world is filled with mystery, meaning and mercy, with wonder, joy and fulfillment; that men have the power to do God's will and that the divine image in

62

which we are made, though distorted, cannot be obliterated."

I cannot forget how Teilhard de Chardin insisted that Christ can be found in the fascinating, demanding, intense, brutal world in which we live. In the turmoil of events Teilhard discovered a great communion with God was possible, a communion with God through matter.

My brothers and sisters, I pray that one day each of you will turn a worn but grateful face to God and murmur: "I did not ask for success; I asked for wonder. And You gave it to me."

They Found God on the Moon

The next time you look up at the moon, think of the astronauts who found God while they were walking on the surface of our nearest neighbor in space.

Of the twelve *Apollo* astronauts who walked on the surface of the moon, six experienced a "powerful mystical experience." They felt "their consciousness being transformed to behold God making all things new." So common did this experience of finding God on the moon become that it was often referred to as "the lunar effect."

"It was an overwhelming experience," said Neil A. Armstrong, the first man on the moon.

Apollo 16 astronaut Charles Duke recalled, "I was overwhelmed by the certainty that what I was witnessing was part of the universality of God."

Walking on the moon was a religious experience for *Apollo 15* astronaut James B. Irwin, who was "deeply moved by the beauty of the lunar mountains and felt the presence of God."

Irwin, who died on August 8, 1991, at the age of sixty-one, said, "I felt the power of God as I'd never felt it before."

A Baptist minister, Roger Lovette, said of the moonwalkers: "It has been interesting to read of the changes that have taken place in the lives of our astronauts when they change their point of view. Out in space, thousands of miles from this tiny planet, things become forever different. Suddenly diapers and braces and car payments and better homes and gardens do not count quite so much. The astronauts have come back to earth to become preachers and poets, novelists and evangelists."

Martin Caldin, a writer acquainted with many astronauts, said, "There has been a tremendous change, very quietly, in the attitudes and lives of men who have gone to the moon, where they can see the planet the way God must have seen it."

The reason for this change, according to the late Dr. Wernher von Braun, is that in space, "evidence of a creator is so overwhelming."

Astronaut James Irwin viewed his moon journey as such an overpowering religious experience that he felt compelled to tell others about it. He retired from the U.S. Air Force and NASA in 1972 and founded High Flight, an interdenominational evangelistic foundation headquartered in Colorado Springs, Colorado. On the speaking circuit, attesting to his faith, Irwin said that his moon visit constituted a "spiritual awakening" for him.

Irwin admitted that when he blasted off for the moon atop the *Saturn V* rocket he thought he was "just going up to get rocks and take some pictures." But, he said, he underwent many changes — psychological, spiritual, and physical.

"When you are on the moon," said Irwin, "and see the earth, it is all so magnificent, for the colors of the earth give a beauty that is beyond description. As we went up from earth to the moon and far out in space, we could actually see the outlines of the continents on earth, and the seas. It is so beautiful and colorful, that I had a feeling over and over again of the glory of God."

5

The World Is Your Birthday Gift

"The world is your birthday gift," said Leo Buscaglia. "It is tied with a ribbon. Untie the ribbon. Look at all the beauty in the world, the glory of sunrise and sunset, the faces of flowers and the faces of children. All yours to enjoy. Yes, life has ugly things also, but concentrate on the wonderful things."

St. Thomas reminds us that in order to become aware of God, we must know his creation. But unless you surround yourself with those things and people and ideas that challenge you or move you or excite you or startle you, you will never be jolted into the radical amazement which engenders an awareness of God. God is waiting to be seen and loved in every moment and place. The purpose of this chapter is to help you focus your attention on some of the gifts of God.

Gravity Helps You to Breathe

Did you ever thank God for the fact that gravity helps you to breathe?

How does this happen?

When you are walking outdoors on a cold winter day, notice that when you exhale, your warm breath rises like a little balloon of condensed moisture.

You are not aware of it, but gravity then pulls down the cold, fresh air with its load of oxygen so that you can inhale it.

Astronauts who are orbiting the earth in their spaceship must take special precautions when they go to sleep. Since the motion of the spaceship cancels out the pull of gravity, their exhaled breath simply stays in front of their face. The colder, fresh air, with its supply of oxygen, is not pulled down to their nose.

How, then, do they overcome this problem? When they go to sleep, they have a fan blowing oxygen against their face.

No doubt you are aware that some twenty percent of the air we breathe consists of oxygen. Did you ever stop to consider how beautifully God arranged for this percentage?

Suppose the air contained ninety percent oxygen. You would not dare to light a match. One spark, one bolt of lightning, and the whole world would burst into flame; in fact it would explode like a bomb!

And what would happen if we had only five percent of oxygen in the air? We would not be able to start a fire. What would we do in January when the wind is a wild wolf stalking the shivering countryside on the paws of winter, running with ice upon his hide?

St. Therese, the Little Flower, loved lightning and thunder. After a thunderbolt crashed in a nearby field, she wrote, "Far from feeling the least bit afraid, I was delighted; it seemed God was so near." Although St. Therese might not have been aware of it, that flash of lightning was helping to keep her alive!

Lightning plays a double role: It can be both a killer and a preserver of life. According to the weather service, lightning kills some 100 to 125 Americans per year. It injures another 1,500 people. Throughout the world there are some 44,000 lightning storms each day and about 100 lightning flashes every second.

The average flash of lightning has about five hundred times as much horsepower than all the American automobiles put together. This vast power, however, is turned on for only about thirty-five millionths of a second.

In a lightning flash you do not see electricity itself — only a burning spark channel or burning air column about an inch in diameter. The searing heat of the flash causes the channel of air to expand or explode with tremendous force. The air wave thus produced pounds against your eardrum to cause the sensation we call thunder.

Even though lightning is at times a fire-belching dragon that scorches the landscape and snuffs out human lives, the fact remains that lightning is responsible for keeping us alive.

How Does Lightning Help to Keep Us Alive?

Without nitrogen, every human being, every animal, and every plant on earth would perish. Nitrogen is an odorless, colorless gas which is a key element in all plant and animal proteins.

Nitrogen makes up about seventy-eight percent of the air we breathe. Some seventy million pounds of nitrogen are in the column of air above an acre of land.

Despite this, no human being or animal can use any of it. To be useful, nitrogen must be "fixed," or combined, with another element.

Here is where lightning enters the stage in the role of hero, the lifesaver and benefactor of mankind. Each time lightning flashes, it combines nitrogen and oxygen with the rain, which carries the "fixed" nitrogen to the ground, where it helps enrich the soil.

Some sixty thousand tons of nitrogen are "fixed" each day. The nitrogen that the rain brings to enrich the soil is ready to serve you. You get nitrogen by eating plants. If you prefer juicy red sirloin steaks, then you get your nitrogen from the Hereford steer that grazed on the prairie grass.

No matter how you look at it, lightning teams up

with raindrops to help transform the air above us into fertilizer for earth-bound plants and prepares the food for us earth-bound people.

We are fed by lightning! Every time we see lightning in action, we are witnessing the continuing miracle of creation. We are watching God at work preparing our groceries for us.

The fascination of life-giving raindrops is brought out by Joseph Cotter, Jr., in his beautiful poem:

On the dusty earth drum
Beats the falling rain;
Now a whispering murmur,
Now a louder strain.

Slender silvery drumsticks
On the ancient drum
Beat the mellow music,
Bidding life to come.

According to Ben Franklin, you prove the wisdom of our loving God every time you lift a cup of water to your lips to drink. Why?

Suppose that the distance from your shoulder to your elbow was much longer, say two feet, and the distance from your elbow to your hand much shorter, say two inches. The forearm would then be too short to bring the cup to your mouth.

Now suppose the distance from your shoulder to your elbow was much shorter, say two inches, and the distance from your elbow to your hand over two feet long. The forearm would then be too long. It would carry the cup quite beyond the mouth. We would have been tantalized.

"Let us adore then," said Franklin, "glass in hand, this benevolent wisdom; let us adore and drink."

Edward Fisher, who teaches at the University of

Notre Dame, informs us that the discovery of design in the universe can lead to a sense of security in the scheme of God's providence.

"As soon as you get a hunch that there is a will of God loose in the universe," says Edward Fisher, "you relax, knowing you are not careening down the mountain road all out of control. All of this is good for mental health and for the life of the spirit."

Magic in a Chicken

Back in the summers of 1926 and 1927, when I worked in Brophy's grocery store in Butte, Montana, you could purchase a chicken one of two ways. Some stores had crates of live chickens. You bought the bird alive, then took it home to kill it and remove the feathers. The store in which I worked had chickens that had been killed, and the feathers plucked, but you had to take the bird home to clean it yourself. You took a sharp knife, opened up the chicken, and removed the stomach and entrails.

Since I was the oldest child in the family, this job always fell to me. To this day I can remember the thrill I experienced when I opened up a hen and found an egg that would have been laid the next day. And then, wonders upon wonder! Sometimes I would find a whole series of eggs in various stages of development. I was amazed to find how the egg progressed from a small, round lump of matter into a finished product neatly packaged by the hen in a shell. "How," I wondered, "did the hen have the 'know-how' to take the grain it ate and transform it into an egg?"

What do you think you would say to a friend who would tell you, "If you want to get a new Dodge 400, simply drive your old Dodge into a hole and cover it over with dirt; return in four months, and behold, you will find a sparkling new Dodge standing there in the sunlight, waiting for you to drive it away"?

"Absolutely weird, ridiculous, absurd," would be your reply.

But consider, now, what happens when you put one watermelon seed in the ground in May. In late August you can return to find, not simply one new watermelon seed waiting for you, but hundreds upon hundreds of them. And these hundreds of seeds are neatly packaged in luscious watermelons attached to the vine that sprang up from the one seed you planted.

The next time you look over a field of watermelons, think of the magic that nature works with black seeds, sun, rain, and the good earth.

Can you plant seeds "upside down"? To find out, plant some bean seeds in flowerpots or tin cans filled with moist sand, soil, or sawdust. Place some of the beans lying flat, in a horizontal position. Place others in a standing, vertical position. Place the rest at different angles. Keep the soil moist and warm for several days.

When the seeds sprout and break through the soil, gently break away the soil from the seeds. What do you find?

You may notice that if a seed was planted upside down, its root came out of the seed pointing to the sky. But the seed could not be fooled. The root then made a neat little turn, and headed the other direction, for the center of the earth. Likewise, the stem first came out of the seed on the bottom side. But it could not be fooled. It, too, made a little turn, and headed for the sky and sunlight.

How does the seed have the ability to know which way is "up" and which way is "down"? Perhaps the answer can be summed up in these lines from the Book of Psalms: "How many are your works, O Lord! In wisdom you have made them all."

Do trees grow on hills the same way they do on flat ground? Keep your eyes open the next time you are in the woods. What do you notice?

On flat ground trees grow at an angle of 90 degrees, or perpendicular, to the ground. If trees grew the same way on the sides of hills, they would be sticking straight out from the steep hills like pins stuck perpendicular into the sides of a pincushion. The tree would be unstable.

When a tree grows on a hillside, cells in the tree produce what is called "reaction wood." This forces the trunk into a vertical alignment and thereby keeps the center of gravity in a relatively stable position.

Trees Are Made From Air and Water!

Since trees put roots down into the earth, it might be supposed that the basic materials come from the ground. To test this theory a Belgian scientist of the seventeenth century, Jan Baptista van Helmont, weighed a tubful of earth and a willow twig which he planted in the tub. Five years later the tree weighed over one hundred sixty pounds. Van Helmont dried the soil and weighed it, as he had done at the beginning of the experiment. The tub of dirt weighed just two ounces less than the original earth. Where did the tree get the one hundred sixty pounds?

Scientists tell us that the raw materials are carbon dioxide and water. Plants absorb water from the soil. The leaves take in carbon dioxide, a substance you exhale into the atmosphere. The green chlorophyll takes from sunlight the energy it needs to change water and carbon dioxide into sugar. As the sugar is formed, it dissolves in the water of the cells.

In some plants, such as sugarcane or onions, the sugar is stored immediately in the stems and leaves of the plant. Most plants change the sugar into starch.

What do you have in common with an elephant, a celery stalk, a lemon tree, and an orangutan?

It may seem strange to learn that all living plants and animals and our own bodies are put together with the same building blocks — protoplasm. "Protoplasm" comes from the Greek words *protos* ("first") and *plasma* ("form"). Whether you refer to your own body, the huge bulk of a whale, or a stalk of celery, each is made of protoplasm. Every living thing contains protoplasm.

Chemists have analyzed materials found in plants and animals. They discovered that protoplasm is made up chiefly of hydrogen, carbon, oxygen, and nitrogen, together with limited quantities of phosphorus, sulfur, and other elements.

When seen through the microscope that protoplasm looks something like the white of a raw egg. It is liquid and can flow. No scientist has been able to tell what makes protoplasm live. Even if he had all the elements that make up such a small plant as a radish, he could not make a radish.

Can 'Worms' Fly?

What would be your reaction if a scientist told you that he had discovered a strange creature that could completely change its appearance several times over in its lifetime?

This creature began life as an egg that hatched into a wormlike creature that ate leaves. Then, this wormlike creature did something incredible. It wove around itself a shroud of silk of the finest texture. It contracted itself within this odd covering and remained without food and without motion for long months. More than anything else it looked like an Egyptian mummy. At last, after the dreary months of winter and the coming of spring, this creature burst its silken "sleeping bag" and took off like a winged bird.

The next time you see a butterfly, remember the life cycle of this beautiful creature.

The multitudinous wonders of the world around us tell us much of God who made them. Speaking of wonders, let us now ponder the following.

Wouldn't it be absolutely miraculous if you could plant flower seeds and then watch the seeds sprout, grow to full height, and burst into bloom — all within two minutes?

You can do almost the same thing if ever you watch time-lapse motion pictures that condense long weeks of slow growth into a time frame of less than two minutes. As you watch in astonishment, the seed breaks through the moist earth, leaps to the sky, then unfurls its dazzling blossoms with the grace and agility of a ballerina pirouetting on a stage.

Flowers are the thoughts of God. It is he who first conceived them, graceful and splendid, with their forms of loveliness and their colors of wonderful beauty. It was he who planned what each blossom should possess of shape, hue, and dimension, what impression each should make on our delighted eyes.

April Magic

When earth distills the deep rich scent of spring, April's lilting voice is heard, a rhythmic ode to beauty. The cone-peaked hyacinth returns to light her blue-flamed chandelier. That magic that is April is captured for us by the poet Robert Browning:

Oh, to be in England
Now that April's there,
And whoever wakes in England
Sees, some morning, unaware,
That the lowest boughs and the brush-wood sheaf
Round the elm-tree bole are in tiny leaf,
While the chaffinch sings on the orchard bough
In England — now!

And after April, when May follows,
And the whitethroat builds, and all the swallows!
Hark, where my blossomed pear-tree in the hedge

Leans to the field and scatters on the clover
Blossoms and dewdrops — at the bent spray's edge —
That's the wise thrush; he sings each song twice over,
Lest you should think he never could recapture
The first fine careless rapture!

And though the fields look rough with hoary dew,
All will be gay when noontide wakes anew
The buttercups, the little children's dower —
Far brighter than this gaudy melon-flower!

According to scientists, it is entirely possible that atoms toppling from the stars have fallen upon planet Earth. These atoms from the stars have been absorbed by the plants and vegetables we eat. Thus, atoms flung out by distant stars in the Milky Way galaxy become part of you!

No longer need you aspire to see stars poised pale on the fringes of space gathering light in frail, pink fire, or rapt in flame and fury. Simply walk to the mirror and gaze upon "animated starlight," alias yourself!

This evening when Chrissy comes walking down the stairs to greet you looking lovely as a convention of angels, you look up in a moment of stunned encounter with utmost beauty. Softly you whisper, "You are out of this world!"

And right you are. The carbon in Chrissy's hair may have come from that royal star, Rigel, a blaze of bluish-white, a jewel made for a queen. The "starlight" in Chrissy's eyes may have come from the seven stars of the Big Dipper whose Arabic names glitter with all the fascination and romance of the mystic East: Alkaid, Mizar, Alioth, Megrez, Phad, Dubhe, and Mirak.

It is stupendous to realize that you and I, made in the image of God, and created only a little less than the angels, have a "space body" made up of the same elements that are found in planet Earth, and in the stars.

Dennis Overbye, a former senior editor of *Discover* magazine, wrote, "I ate a star for breakfast. The star was in the form of a waffle. It consisted mostly of carbon, nitrogen, oxygen and hydrogen, with a sprinkling of other elements. Except for the hydrogen, those atoms had been forged in a star that exploded and died long before our sun and solar system were born. The hydrogen was made in the big bang that allegedly began the universe.

"My waffle and I are star dust. So are we all."

Air — A Bomb Shelter

Do you know that our umbrella of air does duty as a bomb shelter against "space bombs"?

On a clear night when you were outdoors, perhaps you looked up into the sky and saw a shooting star. It looked like a bright, shining arrow shooting across the velvet-black sky.

In truth, the so-called shooting stars are not stars. They are small bits of matter. Some are tiny rocks about the size of a grain of sand. They bump into the earth's atmosphere at a height of some fifty miles. These particles travel at speeds of some forty miles per second. Friction with the air makes them glow white-hot. Trails of gas from the burning rock make a bright, glowing ribbon of light.

Before the tiny rock, or grain of sand, plunged into our atmosphere and made a streak of light, it was called a meteoroid. A meteoroid is defined as a small, solid body traveling in the solar system. Fortunately for us, our air consumes these rocks by friction. The intense heat burns the space rocks to ashes within a stretch of some ten miles. Each day some two tons of these ashes rain down upon us.

When the dust, or debris, left from a shooting star passes through a rain cloud, the tiny iron-ore particles become one of the catalysts for rainmaking. Vapor snatches them. The result? A raindrop with a meteor for a heart! (Meteors are popularly known as shooting stars.)

The next time you stand in a doorway during a sudden shower, put out your hand and bring it back glittering with raindrops. You have just caught a handful of meteors!

The raindrops that splash soft and cool, falling, filling lake and pool, bring iron particles from outer space. As the raindrops seep into the earth, they leave the iron particles that may find their way into your next tomato or potato. You will be eating "stardust" — the remains of a shooting star.

"This most excellent canopy, the air" — to quote from Hamlet — also acts as earth's "thermostat," or "climate control."

If our atmosphere were simply clear, dry air, then all the heat picked up by day would radiate quickly back out into space at night. The setting sun would be the signal that we were about to freeze.

Fortunately for us, water vapor is always present in the atmosphere. Water is, meteorologically, the most important constituent of our atmosphere. It is present up to altitudes of about forty thousand to fifty thousand feet.

This water vapor is a special blessing, indispensable for life on earth. By day this water in the air acts as a "shield" to keep us from being "cooked" by the sun. By night, the water in the air gives off heat it absorbed during the day, and thus acts as a "blanket" to warm Mother Earth at night.

In the good old summertime, young men peel off their shirts to enjoy the sun more "whole-hidedly." Old Sol, besides providing heat waves, also supplies ultraviolet rays that give you that outdoor complexion and make your skin the tone color of smoked elk. But if it were not for our canopy of air, the harmful short-wave emissions from the sun would end our lives with cosmic blasts from this giant X-ray machine in space.

Our air canopy also intercepts the short blue wavelengths from the sunlight to give us the azure "firmament" that makes our sky a wondrous blue and causes the poet to sing:

The sky is a drinking cup,
That was overturned of old,
And it pours in the eyes of men
Its wine of airy gold.

6

Invisible Gifts

You may find it easier to accept the unseen presence of our loving God if you stop to consider some of his unseen gifts.

One of the most dynamic of God's invisible gifts, and one that you make use of every day is electricity.

"But," you may object, "I do see electricity when I look at my reading lamp or the light bulb in the kitchen ceiling."

The light bulbs in your home are called incandescent lamps. The word "incandescent" means "glowing white-hot." And this is exactly what happens. The electricity going through the very thin wires, or filaments, in the lamps makes them glow white-hot so that they give off light as well as heat. The truth is that you never see the electrons forcing their way through the tungsten wire that forms the filament in the lamps.

Perhaps you reply, "I most certainly see electrons in motion when I see a flash of lightning."

When you look at a lightning flash, you do not see electricity itself. All you see is a burning spark channel, or burning column of air, that may be about an inch in diameter or even as thin as a hair on your head. The path of this burning air column may be as long as ten miles. The searing three-thousand-degree heat of the flash causes the channel of air to expand or explode with tremendous force. The airwave thus produced beats against your eardrum to cause the sensation we call thunder. If the discharge is close by, the thunder comes as a sharp whiplike crack.

Enjoying Magnetic Waves

How many hours per day do you set aside to enjoy magnetic waves? If you stop to count the hours you are under the influence of magnetic fields, you will be staggered!

"How can that be?" you say. "I can't be entertained by something I never see. I can't hear it, taste it, smell it, or feel it."

You are absolutely right, since no single sense by itself — not even all five taken together — gives us the faintest clue to the existence of magnetic fields.

The mysterious, invisible world that demands so much of our time and money is that of electromagnetic waves. Think how many hours a day you listen to the radio and watch TV, yet you never see the electromagnetic waves that link your radio and TV to the broadcasting station.

Think of the incredible wonders that surround you every second of your day. No Genie of the Polished Lamp would ever dream of conjuring the magic that electromagnetic waves (radio and TV waves) make possible. As you read this print, these waves are busy. In and out of your room, like morning glories in a trellis, weave the graceful waltzes of Strauss and the lovely melodies of Cole Porter. The voice of Anacani sparkles in soothing rhythm. Your ears can't hear the music directly, so you switch on your radio or TV set. Then, indeed, the electromagnetic waves make true the words of Henry Wadsworth Longfellow:

And the night shall be filled with music,
 And the cares, that infest the day,

Shall fold their tents, like the Arabs,
And as silently steal away.

James Levine, the maestro of the Met, raises his baton, and the New York City's Metropolitan Opera goes on the air. Sound waves are changed into electrical currents by electronic tubes, then flung out into space as electromagnetic waves to be picked up again by your radio and changed back to sound waves. You in Montana, Florida, or Canada hear the same music as the audience in the Met.

Who Hears the Music First?

You may hear the music even before those in the last row of the Met hear it. They hear the melody as it comes to them via airwaves traveling some one thousand feet per second. Radio waves rush the melody to your antenna at the rate of one hundred eighty-six thousand miles per second. With the suddenness of sheet lightning, electrons transform the radio waves into sound. If your easy chair is parked close to the loudspeaker, you may hear Mozart's "The Magic Flute" before the folks in the balcony do.

Four-time Grammy winner Amy Grant steps up to the microphone. Over halfway across the continent, in a tiny farmhouse lost in the vast distances of the South Dakota prairie, a lonely farm wife listens to the ecstatic flight of a human voice that lifts her spirits with the lyric upsweep of song. A senior citizen in a rest home in Phoenix, Arizona, listens in rapt attention as Amy communicates her love for God with poignancy, eloquence, and honesty.

Magic! A song in Radio City is heard around the world. The voice of Luciano Pavarotti becomes as familiar as that of our nearest friend. Even now a voice speaks from the Isle of Manhattan. A hundred-thousandth of a second later it is over the skyline of St.

Louis. Now it sings its way across the snow-capped Continental Divide just east of Butte, Montana.

Music sweeps you in its arms in the graceful waltzes of Strauss, or swirls you in the fiery energy of the Mexican hat dance. Gypsy campfires dance against the night, and your pulse beats high with strange, brooding, wistful emotions. You stroll down mountain pathways where the sound of your footfall is carpeted by pine needles, soft, thick, and resilient as a Persian rug. Or you stand alone on a mountaintop and talk to God.

Voices From the Moon

In September of 1927 I began my first year of high school in the copper-mining city of Butte, Montana. If someone had told me at that time that one day I would sit in a living room and listen to men speaking to me from the moon, I would have thought the idea as fabulous as a fairy tale from the lips of Hans Christian Andersen.

Thanks to the magic of electromagnet waves, I did more than listen to men speaking to me from the moon. I watched them as well. Never will I forget that Sunday afternoon, July 20, 1969, when I was visiting with my parents at their home in Omaha, Nebraska. I sat with them in front of the TV and thrilled to see Astronauts Neil Armstrong and Edwin Aldrin become the first men to set foot on the moon.

"Television" comes from the Greek word *tele* (meaning "far" or "far off") and the Latin word *videre* (meaning "to see"). When you relax in front of the TV set in your home, "you see from a distance."

The most astonishing "far-off" viewing I enjoyed was during July of 1981 when the first *Voyager* spacecraft, traveling at fifty-five thousand miles per hour, made a flyby of Saturn, the ringed planet some eight hundred eighty-six million miles from the sun.

As *Voyager* brushed past the ringed planet, it gave us the best pictures yet of that strange and wondrous world. *Voyager* brought us to a far-off realm in the solar system never before seen with such glittering clarity.

One scientist watching the pictures coming from *Voyager* said, "We have learned more about the Saturn system in the past week than in the entire previous span of recorded history."

When seen through a telescope the rings of Saturn look like washers encircling a ball. *Voyager* gave us a new look at these rings. Before the coming of *Voyager* the rings seemed to be neat circles, six in number, with open gaps between them. *Voyager* showed the rings to be very complicated.

There are rings within rings, upwards of one thousand of them. There are hundreds of smaller rings, or ringlets, mixed in between big rings. One of the big rings, known as the "F" ring, separates into three separate bands. These bands intertwine among themselves to form a braid.

The gaps are no longer empty. The more detailed the pictures, the more the gaps seem to be filled with material.

Some rings had patterns that looked like the spokes of a wheel. Others whirled around Saturn in off-center paths like the grooves of a record that has slipped its spindle. The rings stretch out like the grooves in a phonograph record. They measure more than six hundred fifty thousand miles across.

My hope is that this chapter has alerted you to the invisible, almost magical world in which we live. May you come to realize that every second of your day you are surrounded by invisible gifts that speak to you of God's love.

The next time you switch on your radio or TV, remember to breathe a prayer of thanks to God for his invisible gifts.

7

Vagabonds of the Sky

Did you ever look through the window to find breakfast floating through the sky? Golden pancakes smothered in maple syrup and flanked by coffee brisk as a samba?

This very thing is happening, and more! Clouds put tea in your teacup and soup in the pot. They gurgle with excitement as they leap from the kitchen faucet. You yourself, in fact, are a condensed cloud. Seventy-five percent of your body is water. The teardrops washing your eyes were brought by cloud express, perhaps from the Caribbean, parachuted by raindrops on a Montana mountain peak, splashed down the Continental Divide in singing rivulets, rolled in the mighty waters of the Missouri and Mississippi, and tunneled through blocks of iron pipe to greet you with the tang of the sea and the smile of the sky.

That drop of water — gift of deep ocean and high wide sky — is a liquid package sent air express via nature's cargo ships, the clouds.

Clouds put watermelons on the table, and ice to cool them. Clouds — the type squeezed in living, tortuous, superheated steam tornadoes — beat against the hot blades of a turbine and roar into a crescendo of power to turn a dynamo and furnish kilowatts of electricity for your community. Without these harnessed hurricanes of angry steam there would be no Sunday-night movie, no radio, no television.

Operation Raindrop

When roguish winds unfurl a blanket cloud across the sky and peg it down on the horizon, like a circus tent stretched tight by giant hands, perhaps you pucker up like a persimmon and exclaim, "Rain cloud, go away. I'm going on a picnic with Becky today and don't want dark clouds ruining my parade in any way."

Operation Raindrop may moisten your picnic and dampen your rye sandwiches, but it is essential. It puts the splash in your swimming pool and sparkle in your glass of ale. It chases dirt down the drain better than Ajax and keeps your face from looking like a potato patch. It cleans your teeth and washes your socks. It turns powder-dry cement into hard concrete, proudly to span rivers with graceful bridges and link cities with highways of commerce.

If there is a cloud on your horizon, don't gloom up and splash tears of regret. Rather give with the "Hallelujah Chorus" and thank God your groceries for tomorrow are floating in the sky of today.

Without the ocean in the sky you would dehydrate like a California prune. You would turn bone-dry as Death Valley and lively as a mummy. The wind-leathered, sunburned farmers in the Dust Bowl of the 1930s knew the value of a cloud. They sank to their knees in choking dust and prayed for a white-winged messenger of mercy to coast in with its precious cargo of desperately needed water.

Tennyson spoke of "the island valley of Avilion, where falls not hail, or rain, or any snow. Nor ever wind blows loudly." This would be a peaceful land, indeed, until the village well went dry, the cows went dry, and you developed a burning thirst like a camel just in from a forty-day trek across the scorching sands of the

African desert. About this time you would begin to scan the horizon with eagle-keen eyes for feathers of clouds. When the eager longing for a cool tall drink got the better of you, you would call in the "fly boys" and ask them to take to the skyways in their project cirrus to dust the atmosphere with dry-ice pellets in an attempt to coax moisture from the stubborn sky.

How Valuable Is a Cloud?

Captain Eddie Rickenbacker and Lieutenant James Whittaker are two men who learned the value of a cloud. On October 18, 1942, as their Flying Fortress roared through the sky high over the Pacific Ocean, the gas supply gave out and their B-17 had to crash-land in the blue waters of the Pacific.

Eddie Rickenbacker and crew took to the rubber lifeboats, and there began a terrible ordeal of twenty-three days. Waves tossed them about like driftwood; sharks followed them day and night; the blinding sun beat down from copper skies until their skin was raw and painful to the touch. In his book *We Thought We Heard the Angels Sing*, James Whittaker mentions that on their thirteenth day of utter desperation, the exhausted men noticed a rain cloud moving across the sea. They prayed as they never prayed before. They did not ask God for rare rubies, glittering diamonds, or sparkling opals. They prayed for something of greater value. They asked for the gem of the sky — a raindrop.

In words simple and direct as an arrow, Lieutenant Whittaker tells us how he prayed. "I talked to God as I would have to a parent or friend. 'God,' I prayed, 'You know what that water means to us. The wind has blown it away. It is in Your power, God, to send back that rain. It is nothing to You, but it means life to us.' "

Whittaker went on to say, "There are some things that can't be explained by natural law. The wind did not change, but the receding curtain of rain stopped where it was. Then, ever so slowly, it started back toward us — against the wind. It moved back with majestic deliberation. It was as if a great and omnipotent hand was guiding it to us across the water. We caught a great store of water, and rejoiced as the cool deluge flooded down our bodies."

In this simple, stirring account, we have the experience of men face-to-face with reality. They came to appreciate a cloud for what it really is — a gift from God that makes life possible.

Whence Come the Clouds?

You may ask, "Where do the clouds come from?" The answer is simple: A beam of sunlight sparkling over the aquamarine waters of the ocean is the magic wand releasing soft vapors and sky-born mists. Higher and higher they climb, these invisible ghostly mists. Far up in the sky they join hands and condense to form great misty masses, castles in the sky and pinnacled cathedrals rising from the wide, blue yonder. You can imagine fairy music floating from their spires, as though the heavens heard and understood the faint and lovely call to morning worship in the living church of God.

As you watch, Icarus spreads his wings. A Colossus strides across a bay. Now the darlings of the sky pirouette and swing in ballet dances on the vast blue stage. Like legendary ships on sapphire seas, stately galleons sail beyond tomorrow's sunset, carrying our imagination beyond the utmost bound of human thought.

From the Gulf of Mexico, out of the Atlantic, and in from the Pacific come cargo trains of the sky, pushed by tireless switching engines — the winds. Round the clock they roll, freighting precious cargoes of H_2O and keeping their rendezvous in the sky for a date with destiny.

Science labels these exploded cotton balls as cumulus banks, thunderheads, breeders of storms, and lightning bolts.

Clouds are God's answer when you pray the "Our Father" and request, "Give us this day our daily bread."

Clouds are more than our ever-redeemed promise of daily bread. Every cloud has a silver lining. Clouds put silver dollars in the pockets of farmers, ranchers, and dairymen. If you live in a frame house, clouds built your house. If you live in a brick apartment, clouds cemented the bricks together. Raise a cup of water to your lips: A sparkling, condensed cloud poises on tiptoe to jump down your throat!

Did you ever think of the number of clouds it takes to put the water in your coffee? A cloud big as a moving van has only two tablespoons of water. To give you a bath requires a cloud one quarter of a city block long and as high as a fifteen-story hotel.

In a small rainstorm as much as three hundred twenty billion gallons of water tumble from the bomb bays of the clouds. Along the Wynoochee River in Washington the average rainfall is one hundred fifty inches. Luckily for the natives, this water isn't delivered in one splash; otherwise they would need a new roof job on their penthouses. If rain turned first into ice and then slipped off the clouds in ten-ton chunks, imagine the appearance of your city.

A lonesome cloud floating high in the sky may not look like an emblem of industry, but don't let the innocent-looking traveler in the sky fool you with his bland appearance. The fluffy white vagabond and his cohorts dug the mile-deep chasms of the Grand Canyon and carved the valleys of the world.

These vagabonds of the sky have picked up the shifting weight of pressure-heavy oceans and hurled them down again upon the land, only to have the rivers return to the sea and repeat once more the endless cycle. King Solomon said, "All the rivers flow into the sea; yet the sea is not full; unto the place whence the rivers come, thither they return again." Back into the mountaintops and the high places of the Continental Divide they go, transported by the clouds.

Clouds did more than provide the water that carved out the Grand Canyon. Clouds paratrooped feathery snowflakes that massed huge glaciers, crushing and grinding their way toward the equator during the Ice Age.

Amazing Snowflakes

When King Winter jumps down from the Northland and sifts the snow on the mountains below, while their great pines groan aghast, you may not see much beauty in the blizzard; but the truth is that each snowflake is a work of beauty, flawlessly arranged and perfectly balanced in every part.

A snowflake may be a star, a wheel, or a pointed octagon. If you were making snowflakes, you would no doubt punch them out on an assembly line like tacks. Not so the good Lord God. Each snowflake is uniquely original, distinct in design from all others of its class. Marvel mounts on marvel when we realize that on any winter day billions of these exquisite designs are fashioned and scattered wholesale. Pell-mell they fall on Main Street and Yellowstone Park. High up on the sundown side of the Continental Divide and across the prairies of Kansas fall billions of these sky gems, fashioned for the sheer delight and glory of the Most High.

No two snowflakes have ever been found that are exactly alike. Snowflakes, even though there are millions of them, never take the same design; their varieties are amazingly infinite as the meadows of heaven. Over one hundred thousand separate snow crystals have been recorded.

Wilson A. Bentley of Jericho, Vermont, has collected photographs of snowflakes as a hobby for forty years; he boasts of five thousand unduplicated designs. No wonder a poet wrote:

> God loved a lonely raindrop
> And drew it to the skies;
> He tenderly caressed it
> And wiped its tear-dimmed eyes.
>
> He decked with airy lightness
> Its little form so trim,
> And gave it for its play land
> A fluffy cloudlet's brim.
>
> To magic crystal whiteness
> It changed at His command;
> Reflecting God's perfection
> It fell from out His hand.

Glaciers nestling in the Olympic Mountains of northwestern Washington, icebergs floating in the Bering Sea, scalding geysers bubbling in Yellowstone National Park, even Old Faithful leaping one hundred fifty feet into the Wyoming ozone — all these are grandchildren of the clouds.

Niagara Falls is but a foster child of the clouds that float on high. Over the hills and the rills, over the crags and the plains, the clouds roll on. The fragile magic of their tapestry weaves blossoms in the sky and spins shadows on the earth.

At their whim the forest glooms at the approach of dashing rain, and then laughs again when the leaping sun appears. They stiffen the Great Plains in snowdrifts. They cellophane the aspen tree with ice; they lay their finger on the lips of the mountain stream and it sings with joy.

Clouds mark the tempo of our lives. Sometimes the music is beaten out on the ringing anvils of the sky as the mighty blacksmith of a storm forges lightning bolts and hurls them across the dark, forbidding ramparts of a thunderhead. Startled trees link arms against the anvil chorus in the sky, and the prairie grass bends low, marcelled by fingers of the storm.

The theme of a storm-swept, lightning-riven sky is one of grandeur. The sky becomes alive with things sacred and unknown. No wonder Lord Byron wrote:

Most glorious night!
Thou wert not sent for slumber! let me be
A sharer in thy fierce and far delight, —
A portion of the tempest and of thee!
How the lit lake shines, a phosphoric sea,
And the big rain comes dancing to the earth!
And now again 'tis black, — and now, the glee
Of the loud hills shakes with its mountain-mirth,
As if they did rejoice o'er a young earthquake's birth.

When clouds part hands to let the sun pour nuggets of gold at our feet, our hearts leap up like an antelope and race with delight. April shakes out her rain-drenched hair, and in the tinkling music of a stream we catch an echo of the hidden laughter of a silver cloud. "Like a glow-worm golden in a dell of dew," rain-awakened flowers dot the meadows with pinpoints of shimmering color.

In that hushed and breathless moment when day is almost done, clouds descend the stairway of the sky to mingle with the mountain peaks. Beneath the scarlet banners of a fading sky, shadows deep and blue creep out from the foothills. Quickly they climb the jagged heights. High on a fortress peak, dark shadows clasp the bright red Indian robes of twilight and fold them in a crevice of the night.

As you watch, the words of Psalm 19 come to your mind: "The heavens declare the glory of God, and the firmament proclaims the work of his hands. Day unto day heralds the message, and night unto night makes it known."

8

How God Uses Your Exhaled Breath to Make Apples

A deadly fascination held me rooted to the spot. I gazed in horrified amazement at the potlike utensil in which human beings once were cooked before their steaming flesh was served to the king.

It was my last day in the fabulous Fiji Islands. I was walking through the unique historical museum in Suva, the capital.

The Fiji Islanders make no bones about their history. They give you the naked truth, and let you see for yourself the souvenirs of the distant past when the Fiji solution to the population explosion was to eat your way out of it.

A tourist brochure states bluntly: "At one time the Fiji Islanders were eating each other out of existence."

Let me hasten to add that you don't have to fear "going to pot" if you visit the Fiji Islands today. You won't find hungry natives turning a questioning gaze your way, wondering how many calories you will furnish for Sunday dinner.

The natives today have long left their rugged past and are among the most wonderful people in the world. I found them most friendly, cooperative, kind, and courteous.

On my first afternoon in Suva, I was walking down a tree-lined street leading into town when I fell into conversation with a Baptist minister. He was a native Fiji Islander endowed with a powerful physique; moreover, he boasted handsome, rugged features and thick, bushy hair. His command of English was precise and tailored.

When we reached the downtown section of town, my newly found friend invited me to pause at a refreshment stand that opened onto the street. The pause that refreshes in Fiji is not a Coke but a dish of Jell-O and ice cream, in the proportion of about three parts of Jell-O to one part of ice cream.

The day following my walk with my friend the Baptist minister, I experienced still more of the gracious hospitality and thoughtful kindness of the Fiji Islanders when I took the famous "Colooloo Cruise" to the placid waters and coral-fringed lagoons of Suva harbor.

The view of the coral through the glass-bottom boat was breathtaking in its beauty, but even more impressive was the friendship and cordiality extended to the passengers by all the crew. When we docked in Suva that evening, I felt as though I were bidding "Adios" to longtime family friends, rather than to crew members I met for the first time just a few hours earlier.

Where Would You Meet a Cannibal?

Since you won't be able to find a cannibal by taking a Qantas Airways to the storied lands of the South Seas, just where will you go to meet one?

The answer? Simply walk over to your mirror, and you will find one — looking you straight in the face!

"There must be a hideous mistake!" you insist. "What I see in the mirror is my calm, sweet, rational self. And I most definitely never ate anyone. I never took a bite out of my neighbor or even out of myself."

All true, but did you ever stop to consider the "magic"

in your breath? Each time you exhale, you are giving plants the materials with which to build more apples, more oranges, more radishes.

This breath-building operation requires two most important things: sunlight and chlorophyll. When the golden rays of the sun shake hands with the green coloring matter, or pigment (the chlorophyll in a leaf), green magic is in the making.

The carbon dioxide you exhale is taken in by the leaves. The oxygen is returned to the air for you to breathe again. The carbon is combined with water to make apples, oranges, radishes, and cucumbers.

While we take oxygen from the air and exhale carbon dioxide, plants, on the other hand, absorb carbon dioxide and give off oxygen.

What has all this to do with your being a cannibal? Simply this: The apple you eat today may contain atoms of carbon you exhaled last summer. Thus, atoms that once were part of your body, you are now eating. In this sense, you are "eating yourself."

Some of the atoms in the bread you are eating today may once have been in the body of King Tutankhamen. The air is filled with carbon atoms exhaled by millions of people. Plants take in these carbon atoms to make food. This is the so-called "carbon cycle."

This means that each slice of orange you eat, every radish, every banana, is built from atoms that at one time or another were most likely a part of some other person!

Some folks imagine that the atoms used in the construction of their bodies are "fresh" and "new" and never used before in the construction of any other living body.

The down-to-earth fact is that our bodies are built from "secondhand" atoms that may have been used over and over again by many people, animals, and plants.

Until now, perhaps, you thought of your body as your

very own personal possession. It all belongs to you, you alone, and no one else. It is strictly private property. You don't have to share your molecules with anyone. You are a permanent fixture, like the Rock of Gibraltar or Mount Rushmore in the Black Hills of South Dakota.

You Are a Jug of Water!

If someone called you a jug of water, you would object and reply that you are an individual of distinction, a child of God, an heir of heaven above, and that you have a soul that makes you more precious by far than diamonds and rubies.

All true, but the fact is that your body is about seventy percent water. One third of the water in your body is in the blood and other body fluids. The remaining two thirds is found within the billions of tiny cells that make up living tissue.

There is no such thing as a truly "fresh" molecule of water, if by the word "fresh" you mean one just manufactured and never used before.

The water you drink is as old as the hills. The water in your glass is older than the pyramids, older than the dinosaurs.

It is true that water is made undrinkable by ocean salt and it may be polluted by wastes poured into streams, but let it evaporate into the atmosphere, and it becomes clean and refreshing again.

Water is one of the items in nature that can be used over and over again. Did it ever occur to you that you may be bathing in the same water that sparkled in the marble baths of ancient Rome?

The water in the clear pool that mirrors your reflection on a summer's day may once have rippled to the touch of St. Francis, who called it "Sister Water."

When you turn on a faucet, you are getting water from the ancient seas, final source and reservoir of earth's water. This means that the water you drink today, you may drink again in years to come. If not the exact cup full, at least some of the same molecules.

A water molecule is exceedingly well traveled. The rain running down your windowpane may have flowed in the Thames a hundred years ago. It may have tumbled down the Feather River Canyon or splashed down the sundown side of the Continental Divide. Water is not used up; it is simply changed from one form to another.

The water you sip today may once have passed the parched lips of a Crusader or lapped the boards of Noah's ark!

Are You Related to Cleopatra?

Some of the water molecules coasting through your bloodstream this very moment may once have flowed through the veins of Cleopatra as she drifted down the Nile. Perhaps some of the water molecules in your head once slaked the thirst of a mighty African elephant as it drank by a river's edge in the dark, moist jungle.

Molecules in your right hand may once have been in the hand of Alexander the Great or Richard the Lion-Hearted of England. Through water molecules, you are linked to the great people in history.

You don't belong entirely to yourself, You are "part" of others. There is no such thing as "private water" which is "yours only." Through water you are united to the whole human race, plus, no doubt, a few zebras and roosters!

Some people may find it somewhat humiliating to realize that we cannot call our bodies truly our "own." We may be called "cannibals" to the extent that our bodies are made of "reused" and "reusable" molecules forever "on the go" — molecules that have been part of other people in the past and will be part of still other people in the days to come.

This "ever-changing" habit of our water molecules

should give us a sense of unity and close association with all the world, and the people thereof.

Thanks to carbon and water, we are made a cosmic family. We all become "cousins." Since we take turns sharing the same molecules, I'm happy to claim you, along with Perry Como, Bob Hope, and Debbie Reynolds as my "water-filled," "carbon-swapping" cousins.

Religion is not alone in proclaiming the universal brotherhood of mankind. Science also brings home the same fact by showing us that we all share the same molecules.

It is interesting to note that the "universal brotherhood" of mankind was stressed by Astronaut William Anders upon his return from the moon. He emphasized the fact that his view of the earth from the moon made him aware "that we are all brothers — riders together on a small planet."

We are "riders together" who share with one another the same atoms and molecules. By means of shared molecules, God has made us one brotherhood, one family.

9

He Who Is Mighty Has Done Electrifying Things for Me!

Did you ever send a current of electricity racing to the brain of your friend? Are you aware of the fact that all your knowledge of the great, wide world around you comes to your brain as electric currents?

If all this sounds confusing, then stop to consider some of the miracles that take place every day within your body. If you come to realize these miracles, you will come to love and praise God for his marvelous concern for you. With our Blessed Mother, Mary, you will exclaim, "He who is mighty has done great things for me."

It may come as a surprise to realize that you and I are much like a king who lives in isolation behind the stone walls of his castle. He has to depend on nimble messengers to bring him news about the great, wide world that stretches beyond his castle walls.

The most kingly portion of our body, our brain, is locked up in silent darkness behind the bony walls of our skull. It has to depend on the five senses to bring information about the world that throbs with excitement all around us.

"Nothing is in the intellect," said the ancient Greek philosopher Aristotle, "unless it has first been in the senses."

At birth our minds are absolute blanks — chalkboards with nothing on them. If we were born blind, deaf, and without the cooperation of the five senses, we would live in a world of deathly silence, stifling blackness, and utter void. Not a single idea would ever brighten the long night of our days.

The Eyes Have It

The most important of your senses are your eyes. They bring you eighty-three percent of your knowledge, and guide you through ninety percent of your actions.

What miracles lurk in your eyes! One glance from the one you love can set your heart drumming like pony feet on the hard, dry earth of fall. A single gaze sharp as a sword tip or soft as candle flame sends heat lightning quivering through your pulse, thunder pounding in your veins. No wonder the poet says of love, "It is a flame a single look will kindle, but not an ocean quench."

Eyes, like twin stars sparkling with love-light from heaven, are mirrors of the soul and a gateway to paradise.

A fleeting glance can say so many lovely things. With your eyes you can throw a kiss across the room. Eyes telegraph messages that have no words. They semaphore coded dispatches and relay subtle changes and tempos of the spirit.

No camera can equal your eye, one of God's greatest gifts to you. Your eye is a super-camera, snapping pictures and relaying them to your brain faster than any telephoto news service ever dreamed of. No Canon, Olympus, or Nikon has so many built-in foolproof attachments.

Every second of your wide-awake hours, your living camera is taking motion pictures in flaming Technicolor and CinemaScope. Free of charge, you have continuous programs featuring glorious sunsets, starlit skies, and the faces of loved ones.

The retina in your eye corresponds to the film in a

camera, but it is far better than any man-made film. The retina is a living tissue, a collection of cells. About one hundred thirty million cells make up the retina of just one eye.

There are different kinds of retinal cells, but all are photosensitive, that is, sensitive to light. Each is like a tiny chemical laboratory. When struck by light, the chemical composition of the cell changes. This chemical change in turn excites a connecting nerve and a nerve impulse is sent through the optic nerve to the visual center in the brain. Here the nerve impulse, which is electrical, is interpreted as light.

Oddly enough, the brain itself never directly experiences the energy form we call light. The brain rests in perpetual darkness inside your skull. But its response to the photochemical reaction of retinal cells produces the visual impressions we call sight. Sight may be called the response of living tissue to light energy.

Your Eyes Change Light Into Electricity

Your eyes are really photoelectric cells that change light into electricity! What marvels lurk in your eyes!

Strangest of all, perhaps, is the fact that your brain does not "see" the picture on your retina. The light hitting the retina is changed into electricity. This electricity rushes to the brain through the optic nerve, and then, somehow, in a most mysterious fashion, the brain takes these "electrical signals" and "translates" them into pictures.

In a certain very true sense, we "see by electricity."

Thanks to those photoelectric cells, your eyes, you can step where stars are strewn, pace the cold black desert dune of space, meander on to the moon, and race back to planet Earth.

You can rush to meet the morning as dawn races over the hill when all the world is music in a day in

June. As you drink the elixir of silence, you can see day being born anew. You revel in dawn's enchantment and the glory of the sky.

In October you can see the scarlet maple, bursting into flame, and watch the orange mittens of the sassafras shaking their vivid gold on those who pass.

Like Henry Wadsworth Longfellow you can watch "the hooded clouds, like friars, tell their beads in drops of rain."

According to Nehru, we live in a wonderful world that is full of beauty and charm and adventure. There is no end to the adventures that we can have if only we seek them with our eyes open.

John Masefield informs us that he had seen dawn and sunset on moors and windy hills, and seen strange lands from under the arched white sails of ships; but the loveliest thing of beauty God ever showed to him were the eyes of the woman he loved. No wonder that Ben Johnson penned these immortal lines to Celia, "Drink to me only with thine eyes, and I will pledge with mine."

Sweet, Silent Rhetoric

The sweet, silent rhetoric of persuading eyes is illustrated by Irving Stone in his book *The Agony and the Ecstasy*. He puts these words on the lips of Michelangelo: "I do not aspire to be a talker." The beautiful Contessina replies, "Then you should mask your eyes." "What do they say?" asked Michelangelo. "Things that please me," came the reply.

One big difference between our eyes and our ears is that we can close our eyes and shut out the world of light. We can't close our ears. Since our ears are always open, we can use an alarm clock to pull us out of dreamland.

When the gong hits the bell on the alarm clock, the metal vibrates, or moves back and forth. Vibrating objects are the source of sound. The bell pushes against the air and sets tiny particles of the air into motion. This motion, or vibration, of the air is what we call sound. The moving particles of air hit your eardrum and make it vibrate.

The eardrum is just that: a tiny, drumlike skin, or sensitive membrane, that separates the outer ear from the middle ear. When sound waves strike the eardrum they cause it to move, or vibrate. The eardrum sets into motion three small bones, the ossicles, in the middle ear. These are the hammer, the anvil, and the stirrup, the three smallest bones in the body.

Extending from the inner surface of the eardrum to another membrane that covers the opening between the middle ear and the inner ear, these three bones form a bridge across the middle ear.

Inside the inner ear is a somewhat snail-shaped tube, the cochlea. It contains a fluid and the tiny hairlike endings of the nerve that brings messages to the brain.

As the stirrup vibrates against the membrane covering the oval window, these vibrations are passed to the fluid in the cochlea. The endings of this nerve change the movements into electrical signals which are sent to the brain. These electrical impulses are interpreted by the brain as sounds.

A poet tells us:

God wove a net of loveliness
Of sun, and stars, and birds,
But made not anything at all
So wonderful as words.

No wonder Cyrano de Bergerac looked up at Roxane in the balcony overlooking the jasmine garden and said, "A voice breathed your soul to me. With words you revealed your heart. Now that image of you which filled my eyes first — I see better now. Your name is like a golden bell hung in my heart, and when I think of you, I tremble, and the bell swings and rings . . . Roxane! . . . Roxane! . . . along my veins, Roxane!"

How truly strange and marvelous that emotions quivering with desire, ideas dynamic as a *Saturn V* rocket, thoughts subtle as cosmic rays, can be caught and put into words — sound waves, matter in motion, molecules on the go! And in the cochlea these vibrations are changed into electrical impulses.

"At the sound of your voice," sang Mario Lanza, "heaven opens its portals to me." And Reginald Holmes reminds us that with all of the wonders that God has bequeathed us, there's nothing that thrills like the magic of sound, especially when willing lips say, "I love you."

Your ear brings you the sound of the voice of the one you love. Her voice is like a benediction, a reprieve from loneliness, and the joy you wish of Paradise. Her laughter is as delightful as a carillon of bells in an ancient, lofty tower; her song as joyous as the little winds that run on amber feet across the seas of wheat fields in the sun.

Do you know of anything as powerful as words — warm and golden in whispered confidences, steely and thunderous in harangues, passionate and liquid in supplications, sharp and clawing in invectives, meaningful and creative in lectures?

If you handle words with delicacy and affection you will be king of a jeweled storehouse of language.

The miracle that is speech fascinates Professor Hans-Lukas Teuber, head of M.I.T.'s department of psychology. "What fascinates me is the way that you and I are able to sit opposite each other and make sounds that we receive, decode, process, and than use as a basis for making more sounds. Now that is a real mystery."

According to my friend Father Walter J. Ong, S.J., what words do is precisely annihilate the in-betweenness which separates you from me and me from you. When I speak to you, I am inviting you to enter into my consciousness, and I am entering into yours.

The Gift of Language

Without the gift of language, you and I would wander through life in a fearful silence. It would be difficult to relay thoughts from one person to another.

The gifted writer, the late Dr. Felix Martí-Ibáñez, reminds us that words have another mission in addition to imparting knowledge. That mission is to bring each of us closer to one another and, through dialogue, to turn our cosmic loneliness into companionship.

This is the noblest work that words can do: to act as vehicles of sincere friendship among people.

The simple act of two people meeting and exchanging some commonplace words of greeting forms a link that contributes to establishing the human bases of history, with all its glory and grandeur.

One of the most powerful uses of the spoken word is that of praise. Next to the three little words "I love you," the most popular word in the English language is "Congratulations."

Mark Twain once said, "I can live for two months on a good compliment."

According to the nineteenth-century English essayist John Ruskin, the greatest efforts of the human race have always been traceable to the love of praise. The wise parent makes it a point to compliment a child when he deserves it. Praise from anyone is good, but praise from parents is the best. A child's world is small, and parents are the center.

Praise is the same as saying: "I believe in you. I know you are great. You are capable of wonderful things." That is what we say to God on a deeper level when we praise him. It is one of the highest forms of prayer. It demands self-forgetfulness. It spills over into our attitude toward others, since people are God's handiwork.

When the earth distills the rich, deep scent of spring, and lilacs sway in purple mist, a flower garden is an adventure in fragrance.

The miracle of smell is a most gracious gift of the good Lord that brings us the scent of pine trees in the rain, the pungent aroma of sagebrush, and the lingering fragrance of mesquite.

To make it easy for you to get a fresh start in the morning, there is the invigorating fragrance of coffee waiting to kiss your lips at the dawn of each new day. The bacon sizzling in the frying pan shouts, "Come and get it!"

Smells Can Alter One's Mood

The sense of smell has been called the most richly evocative of our senses, instantly retrieving the dimmest memories, the most distant childhood. Some odors stir up memories so nostalgic that a person's mood can be completely altered.

For one person, a whiff of citronella insect repellent magically capsules a whole north-woods world of pines, birches, throaty loons, and splashing bass.

You may recall with gratitude the appetizing vapors rising from a hot bowl of tomato soup, and the fresh moist nose tingle of an orange.

The reason you can smell bacon sizzling in the frying pan, mothballs in your closet, or freshly cut clover in June is that tiny particles of matter, called molecules, jump up from these various substances, then race through the air to punch you in the nose!

Your olfactory organ consists of two flat membranes, one in the upper portion of each nostril, each about the size of a postage stamp. Sticking out of the membranes, like so many lines on a telephone switchboard, are tiny hairs. When the odor reaches these hairs they send electrical impulses racing along an intricate network of nerves to your brain. There the electrical impulses "light up" a specific code which your brain translates into the appropriate sensation.

What accounts for our attraction to pleasant smells? Science does not fully understand the olfactory organ, or sense of smell. Your nose can receive and sort out odors with a speed and exactness that no scientific instrument or machine can equal.

You notice that a young woman is wearing perfume as sweet as apple blossoms. You may be smelling an amount of perfume so small that no machine known could either find it or tell what it is. Scientists believe that the human nose can pick out as little as one-trillionth of an ounce of a strong-smelling chemical.

It has been said that the nose, not the tongue, really savors your food. A nasally congested person can't tell an onion from an apple, and truffles in aspic at Maxim's cannot be distinguished from fried fish at Joe's Diner. The sophisticated gourmet, like the professional wine taster, appreciates the importance of the nose.

To increase the pleasures of the table many times over, one should exhale very slowly through the nose while eating so that a maximum of precious odor-bearing molecules will reach the pigmented patches of the olfactory organ.

When the aroma from a sizzling steak drifts into your nostrils, the work of your nose is only beginning. Not until you've popped the meat into your mouth does smell come into full play. As you chew, you release odors that rise through the back of your mouth into the inner recesses of your nose, where the olfactory nerve is located. It's there that you discover the delights of a steak that is "done to a turn," and enjoy the tingling tang of root beer.

How overwhelming to realize that your brain never experiences odors directly! All the brain receives are currents of electricity. In some mystic, wonderful manner your brain "translates" these electric impulses into what we call aromas: from peppermint, cinnamon, and clove to jasmine, dill, and rain on a dusty road. In truth, you are "wonderfully made."

The Gift of Taste

Every time you enjoy a piece of lemon pie or sip a strawberry malted milk through a soda straw, you are giving proof that God is sweet, kind, and thoughtful in giving us the miracle that is taste.

Imagine for a moment what it would be like to be lacking the sense of taste. Instead of eating a plate of spaghetti and meat sauce, you could be served a plate heaped high with boiled clothesline and topped with a sauce of chopped wet mop. There would be no difference in the taste — all things would be the same. With your eyes closed, you could not tell the difference between a bar of soap and a cold potato.

The miracle of taste makes the job of keeping yourself alive a pleasant one. Think what would happen if the good Lord would say, "In the future, there will be no pleasure connected with eating. I'm going to supply you with plastic capsules that contain all the food value you need. Just remember to plop a capsule down your throat every morning, noon, and night."

Thanks to your taste buds, the candyman can put delight into your day. The tongue has over three thousand taste buds, each with its nerve connection to the brain. No one knows exactly how these taste-bud receptors work. One theory suggests that particles of food fit into them like light plugs into sockets, closing circuits and sending electrical impulses to the brain. The brain interprets them, then arrives at a judgment: The potatoes need salt, the grapefruit is sour, the strawberry ice cream is sweet.

There are four generally recognized basic tastes: salty, sour, bitter, and sweet. The taste buds sensitive to these various tastes are distributed in a definite pattern on the tongue.

The buds most sensitive to sweet flavors are at the tip of the tongue. You may have noticed how candy tastes sweeter when you lick it, than when you chew it farther back in your mouth. Salt-sensitive taste buds line the front sides of your tongue. A sour taste — lemon, for instance — is recorded by taste buds along the sides of your tongue. Bitter flavors are detected by taste buds on the back of your tongue.

No efficiency expert ever devised an instrument with as many different uses as the one God made when he gave us tongues.

Your tongue is a keel-shaped muscle anchored on one end. It has a greater variety of skills than any other part of your body. It enables you to form those magic messengers in the air we call words — words that can sing, and teach, and sanctify.

To prove how necessary your tongue is for speaking, try keeping your tongue flat on the floor of your mouth and pronounce such words as snap, clack, teeth, and splash.

Your tongue not only channels the voice into articulate speech, it also pilots food between the teeth and steers it to the pharynx. Your tongue helps you eat by forcing the food against your teeth, where incisors grind it under a pressure of 20 to 80 pounds per square inch, and then on to the molars where the pressure rises to 130 to 160 pounds per square inch.

The pressure of your tongue across the top of your mouth when you speak is from 0.5 to 2.3 pounds per square inch. When you swallow, the tongue exerts a pressure of 2.0 to 4.6 pounds.

The tongue's nervous mechanism responds to the slightest pressure so that it automatically clears out of the way of your teeth as you chew.

The tongue can create a lowering of air pressure that

allows the atmosphere to force a malted milk up through a soda straw.

I'm sure that you will agree with me that it is fitting and proper to compose a Canticle of Praise for the Miracle of Taste:

Praise the Lord for ice-cold watermelons, the juicy lushness of ripe peaches, the sting of rhubarb, the zest of dill pickles, and the sweetness of honey flowing rich and golden as liquid sunlight.

Praise the Lord for hot dogs, mustard, relish, and ketchup.

Praise the Lord for golden-brown pancakes, maple syrup, and a glass of cold milk.

Praise the Lord for Mother's apple pie, and the Sunday dinner of roast beef, mashed potatoes, and rich, brown gravy.

Praise the Lord for the taste of fresh corn, the delight of crunchy apples, and the wonder of cider.

Thank you, Lord, for making the job of feeding ourselves a delightful task. How good it is to gather round the festive board with friends in fellowship and contentment! Thank you, Lord, for all the family gatherings that mean so much in our lives.

Your 'Contact' Sense

You are trying to find your way through a dark room. You reach out and touch a hot radiator. Even though you can't see the radiator, you know immediately that it is there.

Touch is the sense that puts us in the most direct contact with the world around us. Our eyes can see stars sparkling on the far side of the Milky Way galaxy. Our ears can hear the distant roar of a waterfall. Our nose can smell bacon frying in a pan. Our taste buds tell us about things that are mixed with the moisture on our tongue. But the sense of touch depends on direct contact.

The nerve endings most sensitive to pressure are close together in the tips of the fingers, the bottom of the thumb, the palm, and the lips. The tip of your nose is also sensitive, as you know when you tickle it with a feather.

Although much about the sensation of pain is still unknown, scientists have found that pain is a coded electrical signal, or impulse, sent to the brain from different parts of your body. The part of your brain that interprets these signals is called the thalamus. This is a Greek word meaning "chamber."

Let's see what happens when you stub your big toe. First, there are nerve endings in the skin called receptors. These nerve endings change the energy of impact, when your toe hits something hard, into a code of electrical impulses. These impulses are then sent by nerve fibers from the toe to the spinal cord. Some electrical messages race up your spinal cord at speeds of up to three hundred miles an hour. Your brain interprets, or translates, these electrical signals as pain.

If someone jabs you in the ribs, the first feeling takes place when the sensory nerves near the surface of the skin send signals to your brain that something has made contact.

These sensory nerves, or touch receptors, are not evenly distributed over your body. A spot on the end of your fingertip or tongue, not bigger than the end of the eraser on your pencil, may have over one hundred receptors. A spot the same size on the back of your hand may have only ten.

How wonderful is the sense of touch! It lets us explore the shape of a tulip's cup and the small cool grape. It brings us the delight of summer sun, and, best of all, it gives us the warmth of friendship when hand meets hand.

How wonderful all our senses are! Our eyes tell us

the shape, color, and size of things. Our ears tell us what sounds things are making. Our sense of smell gives us their aroma. Our sense of taste tells us whether things are sweet, salty, sour, or bitter. Our sense of touch tells us whether things are smooth, rough, hot, cold, dry, wet, slippery, bumpy, soft, or hard.

Most amazing of all is the fact that all this information comes to our brain via currents of electricity.

I began this chapter by asking, "Did you ever send a current of electricity racing to the brain of your friend?" Now you know that you do, every time you shake hands with your friend.

According to Father Pierre Teilhard de Chardin, the sense of touch has an almost mystical quality about it that enables us to reach out and contact God in those we love, and in nature all around us. "Every presence," says Teilhard de Chardin, "makes me feel that you are near me; every touch is the touch of your hand."

10

Your Personal Star

God has given you a personal star. Even though this star is ninety-three million miles distant, it comes down into you in a most amazing manner.

The more you learn about your personal star, the more you will come to realize how much God cares for you. This knowledge will lead to wonder and love. The warm glow of this love will make holy your life.

Did you ever stop to realize that the sun is much more than a celestial companion some ninety-three million miles from our planet?

The sun is your personal star! Without this star you could not wiggle a little finger, whistle while you work, or dance the tarantella.

Even though you may be one mile underground in a tunnel of the Kelley Mine in Butte, Montana, or simply in your own cellar, you may still feel the effect of this star in your life. Simply place your hand on the side of your face. The warmth of your body, the warmth of your blood, is a gift to you from our nearest star, the daytime star we call the sun.

Without energy from the sun you can't give a hoot or a toot. It is energy from the sun that enables you to strum a guitar, pound a drum, or say, "I love you."

Most ancient peoples worshiped the sun because they were aware of a fact that often escapes people today: *All our physical life depends on the sun!*

The sun-bright fact is: You and I are solar-powered! (Solar is from the Latin word *sol* meaning "sun.") Three times a day (or more) we "eat sunlight."

Spicy tomato ketchup, sugary-sweet strawberry malts, the avocado flanking your sautéed salmon steak, hot tamales, and kiwifruit — all are gifts from the sun. Without old Sol, not a solitary radish would break terra firma and reach for the sky. Each lemon, each honeydew melon, is a fresh gift to you from the sun. Every chicken in the pot, every pot roast in the oven, was put there by the sun. If the sun were to go out of business tomorrow, we would have to go space-hunting for another planet on which to grow sweet corn and squash.

The Sun Puts Clothes on Our Backs

Without the sun, planet Earth would be naked as a billiard ball — not a stitch of grass to cover the ground; and we likewise would be bare, for our suits are either taken from cotton fields or lifted off the backs of sheep, who, in turn, munch green grass to make white wool.

Someone has defined a farmer as "a handy man with a sense of humus." But humus would be just that until the sun gives forth with magic, making each green leaf and blossoming bud a private miracle.

Of all things on planet Earth, only plants can capture the energy from the sun and give it to us in the form we need to keep alive. Green plants carry on the most important manufacturing process in the world: making food. What farmers really do is collect solar energy.

The plant material that holds the key to this mysterious food-making process is chlorophyll, a green coloring matter. (The word "chlorophyll" comes from a Greek word, *chloros*, meaning "green.") In the presence of sunlight it manufactures food.

This process of manufacturing food with the energy from the sun is called photosynthesis. "Photo" comes from the Greek word for "light." "Synthesis" means to "put together" or "build." Photosynthesis is "building with sunlight."

When the golden rays of the sun "shake hands" with the green pigment, or chlorophyll, in a leaf, magic is in the making. The plant is packaging energy from the sun.

Every orange is a little CARE package made possible by the cooperation of the sun and the leaves on a tree, a freshly minted gold piece, a gift bursting with energy from outer space. Each Sunkist orange is just that. Each drop of orange juice is "kissed" with energy from your daytime star.

Every leaf on an apple tree is a solar energy collector. A cotton field is a reminder that green leaves are at work so that you may go about wearing captured sunlight, alias a cotton shirt or blouse.

A carpet of golden poppies spread beneath giant saguaros along the Apache Trail in Arizona calls to mind the fact that each poppy is a miner who digs into the arid hills and brings out petaled gold. That petaled gold is freshly minted sunshine served up on a green stem.

An ad for raisins tells us that they are "neat, sweet tiny capsules of sunshine and packed with the energy we need for our daily activities."

People rule the seven seas. They build a Boeing 747 jet that leaps from New York to Paris in six hours. They send a *Voyager* spacecraft out to Saturn to take pictures of its spinning rings. But they cannot make even one little radish! A little blade of green, however, can do just that!

Exactly how this is done is a great mystery. It is a mystery upon which our lives depend. Yet how often do we stop to think of how God is working for us in every green leaf?

A green leaf has more mystic secrets in its fragile

design than all the elves of Ireland that haunt the Lakes of Killarney, or the trolls of Iceland that dwell in the high places east of Reykjavik.

Though delicate as an orchid and lovely as a lily, the blade of green guards its secret with a strength that laughs at the vaunted intelligence of the A-bomb experts. Its secret evades the calculations of slide-rule artists and escapes the jaws of calipers.

Magic! Here is a tantalizing mystery that even Sherlock Holmes couldn't solve. With the searching eye of the microscope and the sleuthing of chemical analysis, scientists have not been able to pry open the secret of the blade of green, to learn its formula, to find out how the energy of sunlight is stored in the sugar which is made there.

Each year the amount of the sun's energy fixed in this fashion amounts to the equivalent of three hundred million tons of coal. We know of no other practical process which can fix the sun's energy in chemical compounds.

Masquerade in Green

In the last analysis, the reason you can walk, talk, and sing is that the sun reaches out through ninety-three million miles of space to catch you in its warm embrace, and kiss you with its life-giving powers — not directly, but in the magic of its masquerade in green.

We can actually measure the amount of the sun's energy captured for us by plants and served up to us on our tables. The heat-producing value of food is measured in calories. A teaspoon of sugar contains 18 calories. An individual serving of Grape Nuts contains 134 calories. A serving of Wheaties has 107 calories.

Most of us are so accustomed to having the sun deposit a fresh day at our doorstep that we take the whole process for granted. We never stop to realize that the nearest star over our heads is giving us this day our daily bread, enriched with energy from on high! Bread — including the brand that "builds strong bodies twelve different ways" — is truly wonderful. It is packed with captured sunlight, energy from a star!

The Indians of the Southwest are well aware of their dependence on the sun. A Navajo will feel perfectly at home shopping in Flagstaff or Winslow, and will barely turn his head when a Boeing 747 cruises through the sky; but when he builds his hogan, the opening will always face the rising sun, for such is the way as well as the thoughts of his people. The Navajo knows — and is grateful — that it is the sun that fills the pods of the mesquite trees with rich and nutritive beans.

Did you ever stop to realize that most of the money you make in your lifetime will be spent on things that come to you from your personal star, the sun?

When you buy a loaf of bread, for example, you are purchasing energy from the sun that was captured by blades of wheat and stored in the life-giving grain.

Did you ever stop to reflect that our immediate body needs are cared for by recent shipments of energy from the sun? The radish you pull from your garden may be considered a "package of freshly minted sunshine." Just before you pulled it, the leaves of the radish were busy capturing energy from the sun and storing it for your use.

If you prefer a hamburger or steak, you depend on still another process. A white-faced cow on a ranch in Nebraska obligingly ate the grass. Then, through the marvelous magic of "the chemistry lab on hoofs" (the cow), the grass was turned into red-blooded steaks. But all the energy to do this comes from the sun!

Can you carry some of the sun in your pocket?

Yes, if you have a big kitchen-size match with a wooden stem. Once upon a time the wood in the matchstick was part of a growing tree. Green leaves on the tree captured energy from the sun and stored it in the wood.

Strike the match, and watch the magic. You are feeling heat from the sun! When the match burns, it releases heat from the sun that was captured by green leaves many years ago. This stored energy was waiting for the moment when you release it. It is "sun energy."

Buried Treasures

Coal, oil, and gas are like the match. They all contain energy captured from the sun.

Ancient swamps and forests were covered over with deep layers of earth. The trees and plants buried under the ground were turned into coal.

Oil and gas are the remains of ancient sea animals that once lived in oceans. They got their energy from plants and seaweeds that had taken in the energy from the sun. When these ancient sea animals died, their bodies were buried under tons of earth. The pressure from the weight of layers of earth turned their bodies into oil and gas. Thus, coal, oil, and gas are all gifts from the sun.

No wonder that coal is called black sunlight and oil is called liquid sunlight.

Even windmills are run by the sun! Winds are due to the uneven heating of our atmosphere by the sun.

The "star that makes our weather" pours forth golden rays of sunlight. The sun's rays warm the earth, and the earth warms the air above it. But all parts of the earth do not receive equal amounts of heat from the sun. They do not warm up at the same rate. This unequal distribution of heat leads to differences in the air above such areas. This leads to movements of air, which we call the winds.

It was the energy of the wind that blew early explorers to our shores. It was wind that filled the sails of ships that brought thousands of people to our land. For centuries the only way people had of traveling around the world was wind power.

Wind power was in use long before our country was discovered. Windmills were used in Europe in the twelfth century. Among other things, they were used to pump water and grind grain.

Whether you drive your Ford Tempo down Highway 81 or play bingo or glide in a sailplane on thermal updrafts, you are doing so, thanks to energy from the sun.

Did you ever stop to consider that your pleasure comes from the sun? Every human activity is simultaneously an activity of solar energy.

Cosmic Gifts

The bread you eat and the coffee you drink resulted from the coming together of unimaginably powerful and diverse forces of sun and water and soil. Every mouthful of food is a cosmic gift. Think how every orange, every ice-cream cone, is deliciously converted into you.

We should learn the truth about our utter dependency on the sun, and then thank God for this golden sphere that speaks to us of our Creator's kindness and care.

The golden alchemy of the sun is captured by K. K. Thompson in his poem "First Easter Dawn":

> Lord, now that spring is in the world and every tulip a
>   cup
> Filled with the wine of Thy great love, lift Thou me up,
> Raise Thou my heart as flowers arise to greet the glory
>   of Thy day,
> With soul as clean as lilies are, and white as they.

G. K. Chesterton reminds us that "sunlight in a child's hair is like the kiss of Christ upon all children."

Sunlight touches everything with its magic wand, and spell-bound hours flower into perfect, golden days when youth and age walk hand in hand through the eternal miracle of spring.

The forest hears again the shy new laughter of a mountain brook; as sleepy trees awake, the remnants of their winter dreams drift by in melting mirrors made of snow.

Adrift in beauty and delight, the days of spring flow swiftly by until, at last, the valleys and the hills are crowned with green, in dedication to the life-giving sun.

The Grand Ganyon

One of the most dynamic and thrilling experiences I ever had of contact with God's beautiful, fascinating world took place on Tuesday morning, August 8, 1961. I arose while it was still dark and walked to the rim of the Grand Canyon to watch the miracle of sunrise.

As the candlelight of dawn began to quiver far to the east, I thrilled to watch a brand-new day emerge from night's black wrapping paper. But I was totally unprepared for the explosion of color.

I looked down into the tremendous chasms of the Grand Canyon and felt as though I were viewing the dawn of creation. From utter voids of chaos and black mystery God was fashioning a Technicolor world of flaming beauty.

As the first rivulets of sunlight trickled down over the eastern ramparts, they flooded the Canyon with dazzling blues that shaded into deep purples. The vast immensity — comparable to a giant Koh-i-noor diamond — throbbed and pulsated with strange, mystic lights shimmering with mystery, fascination, and intrigue.

The seemingly never-ending depths of the Canyon lost themselves in regions of baffling darkness. With a dash of imagination you could picture the caverns under whose secret recesses is fettered the thunder that struggles and howls by fits. Or, perhaps, in these dark, inner regions of the earth were chained fire-spewing dragons from the Land of Oz.

The flanks of the Grand Canyon have been slashed and gouged by the talons of time into such weird shapes and swirling patterns that it could well be the landscape of some distant planet.

As I looked at the scenery below me, I found myself peering down into brooding voids of tumbled space. Autographed by wind and storm, color-splashed cliffs crowd the hush of silent miles. The impact of primitive beauty was overwhelming.

Complete fascination compelled my eyes to take in the bewildering maze of deep abysses, stark cliffs, and twisting, snakelike canyons that vanished in far horizons.

Where streams of sunlight splashed against the sides of the Canyon, the rocks of centuries fanned out into spectrums of color like peacocks on dress parade. Whole mountain peaks rising out of primeval depths exploded in a glare of flaming red, vibrated with periwinkle blue and burnished gold, then subdued into jade green and driftwood gray and sandalwood.

Pinnacles of canary yellow were striped with streaks of Cherokee red, like Indians on the warpath. Far to the north flat-topped mesas and high buttes lost themselves in tantalizing shades of colors that have no name. Here and there sunshine broke in galaxies of diamonds against lofty monoliths and fluted columns that might have been the entrance to the temple of Apollo or Jupiter.

As I lifted my vision from the tremendous voids that tumbled away into mystery beneath me, I noticed that the ocean of purple lights that surged before me was blending like magic into tremulous blues that extended above the Canyon's jagged peaks, then seemed to blend and never end in all of space above.

This was ecstasy and thrill, the heart's swift running out to meet delight — here the vision of a day that would remain forever bright and shining like a dazzling diamond sparkling in the treasure chest of happy memories.

Even the very rocks seemed to echo the words of Psalm 100, "Sing joyfully to God, all the earth; serve ye the Lord with gladness. Come in before his presence with exceeding great joy."

Planet Earth owes its color-splashed fascination to the daytime star we call the sun!

Neither the Grand Canyon nor Mount Rushmore — not even Yellowstone National Park — gives off any color of its own. On a dark night, when low scudding clouds shut out even the feeble light from the stars, you can stand five feet away from a mesquite tree and never see its spring dress of little yellow catkins. A mountain locust, a desert marigold, and a fairyduster are all wrapped in equal blackness. The tiny goldfields weave no saffron yellow carpet, the delicate hyacinth does not parade its beautiful lavender headdress, and the owl cover nods no maroon head.

It is only when the morning sun comes cascading over the eastern horizon that mountains leap and gleam with color, and beauty crowds the hush of desert miles.

It is sunlight that tips the flaming fire in the Indian paintbrush and turns the Montana sky into an immensity of baffling blue, a dome of azure crystal, luminous as a jewel. It is sunlight breaking in galaxies of diamonds against the rippling waters of Lake Michigan that gives it the beauty of sapphire and aquamarine.

It is the sun that bursts the claret-cup cactus into blossoms that make music out of color.

Do you go around dressed in sunlight? The answer is yes if you are wearing a cotton shirt or blouse or slacks. The cotton dress or slacks you are wearing may be a gift from a Pima cotton field in Arizona. You are dressed in "packaged sunlight."

If you are wearing leather shoes, remember that the leather comes from a cow's hide. Depending on how you want to look at your feet, they are wrapped in grass or covered with captured sunlight.

The gasoline you buy for your car is "liquid sunshine." It comes from the remains of marine animals that ate plants that grew in ancient oceans.

When you pay your heating bills in winter, you are paying for the gas that also comes from these same marine animals of millions of years ago.

In most cities in the United States, when you pay your electric bill, the money goes to pay for "buried sunshine" — the coal that was once a tropical forest that absorbed energy from the sun. The coal is burned to furnish the heat to turn water into steam that spins giant turbines. The axle of the turbine is connected to a generator that spins coils of wire inside a magnetic field and thus generates electricity.

How to Put the Sun in a Bottle

Did you ever hear the expression "I'll leave the porch light burning until you get back"?

Actually, the porch light is not burning. The only fire connected with it is miles away. It is in the boilers of the powerhouse where the electricity is being made.

Three fourths of all electrical power in the United States comes from generating plants that burn coal. This is no slow, drawn-out process. One instant a particle of coal is shot into the boiler or furnace. In less than a second the energy of that coal is changed into steam, and then into electricity. Then it races through miles of wire to heat your electric iron, run your vacuum cleaner, and light your reading lamp.

The energy that is running through the filament of your lamp this moment may have been waiting in a lump of coal for millions of years to do its task. In other words, the energy that lights the lamp comes from the sun. So we may say that in every electric lamp we have "the sun in a bottle."

If you live in a house made of wood, then most certainly you are living in a house that came to you from the sun. It was our daytime star, the sun, that made the trees grow that provided the floor you walk on and the roof over your head.

Even if you live in a brick house or one made of cement, you still live in a house provided by the sun. It was the sun that provided the coal and gas that was used to bake the bricks and to make the cement.

Portland cement is not a brand name; it is a type of cement, just as anthracite is a type of coal. There are scores of different brands of portland cement. Portland cement is a mixture of limestone, shale, oyster shells, clay, marl, iron ore, slag, and silica sand. These ingredients, ground up into a very fine powder, are blended together in proper proportions and then heated to a temperature of 2700 degrees or more. The fuel used may be powdered coal, natural gas, or fuel oil.

Transparent Magic!

Scoop up a handful of sand. You cannot see through it. The sand is opaque. Now behold the magic. Melt the sand and you can form it into a windowpane that allows the sunlight to pour like melted butter into your room.

Energy from the sun locked in fossil fuels (coal, gas, oil) provides the heat that melts the sand and turns it into transparent glass.

Every window is a gift to you from the sun, as well as the lens of your camera, your TV tube, and the bottles on your kitchen shelf.

Whether you drive a Ford, Volkswagen, or an Isuzu your car is a gift from the sun. It was the sun that provided the fuel to stoke the blast furnaces that melt the iron ore and shape the steel. Likewise every bridge, every skyscraper with its steel beams, is a gift from the sun, along with your bike and fork and knife.

From the pennies in your pocket to a Boeing 747 jet soaring overhead, the whole world around us reminds us of our cosmic connections. The food we eat, the clothes we wear, the machines we use, our houses and skyscrapers are all — in a very true sense — gifts from the sun.

Every step we take, every breath we draw, is due to the fact that we are truly "cosmic." We are powered by a nuclear power plant some ninety-three million miles over our head. The sun is more than just a heavenly body distant by eight and one-half minutes via light beams. The sun is our daytime star that "gets under our skin" and "keeps us alive."

Did you ever stop to thank God for the many benefits you receive from our daytime star?

You may recall the statement "Whoever stands to watch a sunset, moves in close to God." Listen now as Mr. H. V. Morton describes such a symphony in color:

On a clear evening when the sun is setting below the Atlantic, this hill above Mallaranny, Ireland, might be on the map of heaven. An unearthly beauty pulsates in the air; it is an opalescence which seems to have a music in it, and even if the Angelus bell were not ringing below in the white convent, you would bare your head.

Such a heartbreaking symphony in blue is rarely seen in the world. Standing there, with the gulls crying and the larks shivering in the sky, and wind going through the heather, a man goes cold with the beauty of it, and is glad to be alone.

Then the whole scene fades a tone and the music behind it drops an octave; but all the colour is still there, not departing, it seems, so much as sinking into the earth and withdrawing itself into the sky. You stand watching it with tears in your eyes, the first wind of night touching your hair and cold on your face.

As the great world spins forever down the ringing grooves of change, its unceasing thunder and eternal waves speak to us of the Creator who lights the stars in the heavens and opens the blossom of the hawthorn. Long fields of barley and of rye that clothe the world and meet the sky tell us of him who listens to our most oft-said prayer, "Give us this day our daily bread."

No one can gaze steadfastly into the sun. Its blinding radiance is too overpowering for our weak eyes. But we catch reflections of its beauty in the violet hidden in its dell of dew, in the vivid orange-red mariposa lily, in the stately grandeur of the California redwoods, and in lilacs swaying in purple mist. All this pageant of color, luster, and glory is borrowed from the sun.

We cannot bear to gaze at the sun; its radiance is too keen and strong for our eyes to endure, but we can perceive its beauty in the mirrors of the earth.

We need to develop the application of this metaphor to our knowledge and our love of God. He is the Uncreated Sun of the universe. His power and beauty illumine all creatures, giving them whatever loveliness and lovableness they possess. God is infinitely beautiful and lovable. In him are all blessed traits of amiability and perfection. Whatever we see in his creatures, we may use to help us to conjecture his lovableness.

We may forever increase in the knowledge and love of God by contemplating him in his mirrors of creation. Each creature has something to reveal to us of his divine perfections.

God contemplated his own essence and saw therein all the possibilities of imitating it in creatures. He is the exemplar and model of all created loveliness.

So magnificently does the sun serve as a symbol of

the divine that Christ himself is spoken of as the Sun of Justice and the Light of the World.

St. John, the Beloved Disciple, was the first to catch the symbolism. As the sun is the center of all physical life and energy, so Christ is the center of our spiritual life. He is "the way, and the truth, and the life, the true light that enlightens every man who comes into the world."

The Sun and Christ

During the thirty years I taught physics and general science at Campion High School in Prairie du Chien, Wisconsin, I had a beautiful brass emblem of the sun mounted on the front wall of my classroom, directly above the chalkboard. This gleaming emblem depicted the sun in all its glory with rays of golden light radiating out in all directions. Alongside this emblem of the sun I had an equally large painting of Christ. Calling to mind St. John's thoughts, I informed my students that just as the sun is the source and center of all our physical life and energy, so also is Christ the source and center of our spiritual life.

St. Francis of Assisi possessed an entirely direct love of nature. He believed the words of St. John, "All things were made through him, and without him was made nothing that has been made." In this common relationship with one and the same Father, St. Francis saw all created things as brothers and sisters. It is truly Christian, this outlook, and hence St. Francis turned to all that was lightsome, beautiful, and bright in his surroundings — to light, fire, and running water; to flowers and birds. Every creature was a direct word from God, and he understood God's presence among them.

Above all things, Francis was thankful for the sun. "In the morning," he said, "when the sun rises, all men ought to praise God, who created it for our use, for all things are made visible by it. But in the evening, when it is night, all men ought to praise God for Brother Fire, who gives our eyes light at night. God gives our eyes light by means of these two brothers."

From his hut in San Damiano, Francis arose early and said, "I will for God's honor and for your comfort and the edification of our neighbors compose a new song of praise about the creatures of the Lord whom we daily make use of, and without whom we could scarcely live."

And Francis sat down and thought. After a moment he broke forth with the first words of the song *"Altissimo, omnipotente, bon Signore* (Highest, almighty, good Lord)!" When the song was composed, his heart was full of comfort and joy, and he wished straightaway that Brother Pacificus would take other brothers with him and go out along the highways. Wherever they found themselves, they were to stop and sing the new song of praise, his "Canticle to the Sun":

Highest, almighty, good Lord,
Praise be to Thee for all Thy creatures,
Especially for our Brother the Sun,
Who makes the day, and shows forth Thy light.
Beautiful and radiant is he with great splendor;
To us, he is the symbol of Thee, O Lord.

Praise be to Thee, O Lord, for our Sister the Moon and
    the Stars,
Thou hast set them in the heavens, clear, precious and
    beautiful.
Praise be to Thee, O Lord, for our Brother the Wind.
And for the air and clouds, and all kinds of weather
By which Thou givest life to all creatures.

Praise be to Thee, O Lord, for our Sister Water,
Who is very useful and humble, precious and chaste.

Praise be to Thee, O Lord, for Brother Fire,
By whom Thou givest us light in darkness.
He is beautiful, jocund, robust and strong.

Praise be to Thee, O Lord, for our Mother the Earth,
Who sustains us and nourishes us,
Bringing forth various fruits, flowers of many colors,
And the grass.

Praise and bless my Lord and give Him thanks
And serve Him with great devotion.

The symbolism between the sun and Christ is the reason we celebrate Christmas on the twenty-fifth of December! If this seems strange to you, then read the next chapter for an explanation.

11

December 25th Is the Birthday of the Sun!

Was there a glitch in the computer or was the typesetter half asleep when he or she keystroked the heading for this chapter?

Neither of these. The heading is correct. The reason we celebrate Christmas on the twenty-fifth of December is that this is the birthday of the sun!

If all this confuses you, please read on.

It may come as a shock to learn that we do not know the precise day on which Christ was born. Before the fifth century there was no general agreement as to when to celebrate the birth of Christ. Various suggestions were made, including May 20, April 19, and November 17.

According to many historians, the idea of having a celebration on or about December 25 was born thousands of years before Jesus Christ. It began in Mesopotamia, then journeyed from there to Greece and Rome and up the Danube valley to the warrior tribes of the frozen North.

Many of these ancient peoples were avid students of astronomy, and they knew that toward the end of December was the time of the winter solstice, when the sun dwindled, the days grew shorter, and darkness seemed to be swallowing the earth.

139

The twenty-fifth of December was, by their calendar, the turning point, when the sun began to reassert its power once more and give new promise of fruitful harvests. In Rome it was known as *"Dies Natalis Invicti Solis* (The Birthday of the Unconquered Sun)."

It seemed logical to some Christians to try to "transpose" the feast in honor of the sun to Christ, the "Sun of Righteousness" and "the true Light."

The transition began about the year 354 and took nearly two centuries. Even though all pagan aspects were gone from the Christian version of the feast, some Syrians and Armenians accused the Roman Christians of sun worship!

Acceptance of December 25th as the Lord's birthday gradually came about.

In the year 529 the emperor Justinian declared the day a civic holiday. As centuries slipped past, Christmas gained in increasing importance.

It was in nineteenth-century England — during the golden age of Christmas — that many of our colorful Yule messages and greetings were born. This was the era of "The Merrie Words of Christmasse," when Dickens wrote, "Christmas is a good time, a kind, forgiving, charitable, pleasant time, the only time I know of, in the long calendar of the year, when men and women seem by one consent to open their shut-up hearts freely."

It was of this time that Sir Walter Scott wrote, "England was merry England when old Christmas brought his sports again. 'Twas Christmas told the merriest tale. A Christmas gambol oft would cheer the poor man's heart through half the year."

And Sir Walter Scott knew from history whereof he spoke. In 1644, when Oliver Cromwell and his Puritan followers came into power, they banned the whole Christmastime celebration as "immoral sun worshippe."

The Puritans fell from power in 1660, and Christmas

returned to merry England; but the zeal of the Puritans who fled to America persisted to the latter part of the last century. All Christmas celebrations were forbidden in Puritan colonies, and December 25 was a common workday.

December the twenty-fifth of 1620 was the first Christmas spent in the New World by the *Mayflower* Pilgrims. The day was devoted to hard work. The Pilgrims utilized all their energies felling trees "in order to avoid any frivolity on the day sometimes called Christmas."

On May 11, 1659, in the Massachusetts Bay Colony, the colonial legislature made Christmas illegal: "Whosoever shall be found observing any such day as Christmas . . . shall pay for every offense five shillings," read the law.

'A Popish Frivolity'?

To Robert Brown and his Pilgrim associates, Christmas was nothing more than "a popish frivolity."

Because of its association with pagan festivals of early times, the Pilgrims went so far as to outlaw the color green. Pilgrim preachers used their pulpits to strongly denounce holly and ivy as "seditious badges."

The harsh law banning Christmas lightheartedness remained in effect in Massachusetts until 1681. Christmas that year could be celebrated without dire consequences. Yet the Pilgrim chill on the holiday persisted for another one hundred seventy-five years. Children in that area of New England were still made to attend school on Christmas Day. This rule applied in Massachusetts up until 1856.

Today, thank God, you can celebrate Christmas in Massachusetts without having to pay a penalty of any kind.

Since the sun serves as a symbol of God, the Uncreated Light, it is entirely fitting that God's coming to earth should be spoken of in terms of light. In the second Mass of Christmas we read: "A light shall shine upon us this day, for the Lord is born to us, and He shall be called wonderful, God, prince of peace, Father of the world to come of whose reign there is no end."

And in the third Mass of Christmas, St. John reminds us again that Christ is the real Light that gives light to every person.

Since Christ is the Light of the world, and the sun is used as a symbol to refer to him, it is not surprising that next to the shepherds, the first to adore the Christ Child were fire-worshipers.

From fire-worshiping Persia came the Zoroastrians (or fire-worshipers) whom we call Wise Men, the Magi, whose name for God was Ahura Mazda, the god of light. (When I was a boy, electric light bulbs were spoken of as Mazda bulbs.)

Mounted on their camels with their full-stuffed saddlebags, the Magi had forded the Tigris and the Euphrates, crossed the great desert of nomad tribes, and followed the star of Bethlehem along the Dead Sea.

The Wise Men were not kings, but in Media and Persia, they were the masters of kings. The kings ruled over the people, but the Wise Men directed the kings. They alone could communicate with Ahura Mazda. No king began a war without consulting them. In the name of science and religion they held first rank in the nation.

It was in the cave of Bethlehem that the fire-worshipers found the Light of the world. The tiny Infant Christ is the center of light for all mankind. He is brightness breaking over the darkened minds of humanity. He is the dawn toward which antiquity moved. He is the burning Babe at whose side all our race can warm its chilled hands and freezing hearts.

Is it any wonder that at Christmas the earth breaks into a blaze of lights to honor the Light of the world?

Light symbolizes joy, and joy must fill a world that was dear enough to its Creator to win from him such a beloved Son.

Light symbolizes knowledge, and Jesus came to teach us the most cheerful and encouraging truths: that we are the children of God, and that he loves us like a father.

Year after year, sparks from the cave of Bethlehem enkindle the world in a blaze of Christmas light.

The 'Son' and the Sun

Recently I received a letter from a grandmother who wrote, "When I was young I never thought about the sun, but in the past years it has grown in importance to me. I tell my granddaughter, Kristen, that in years to come when she looks at the sun as it rises, or a beautiful sunset, will she please think of me. Since I am already advanced in years, I don't expect to be here when she grows into womanhood. I can think of nothing more constant and glorious than the sun. It has a tremendous effect on my own daily outlook. If the sun shines I can ignore a lot of little problems. If the sun is hidden and the day is gloomy, I can be very depressed. And I have long been aware of the parallel of 'Son' and Sun. Without either one I would be lost completely."

12

Love Letters From God

Who can begin to tell the story of how great a love can be? The answer? You can. All you have to do is to read the love letters that God sends you every day.

Our minds cannot reach out at present and grasp God in the fullness of his splendor. Only in the dazzling brilliance of the beatific vision will we see God face to face. Though God is not visible to us now, he tells us about himself in love letters.

The love letters God sends us are printed in flaming stars high overhead so that all who see may read. They are inscribed in the fragile beauty of an orchid, emblazoned in the scarlet glory of sunset, and sculptured in the granite upthrusts of mountains rising like arrows into the sky.

The person who looks upon creation as a love letter from God finds God everywhere. In the words of Ralph W. Emerson:

Go where he will, the wise man is at home —
His hearth, the earth; his hall, the azure dome.
Where his clear spirit leads him, there his road,
By God's own light illumined and foreshadowed.

Quiet beaver ponds ringed with solemn spruce, myriads of stars beating with hearts of fire, white and

145

topaz and misty red, the wind whispering its secrets to the treetops — all these are sacramental things to teach the minds of all. Joseph Addison tells us:

The spacious firmament on high
With all the blue ethereal sky,
And spangled heavens, a shining frame,
Their great Original proclaim.
Th' unwearied sun, from day to day,
Does his Creator's power display,
And publishes to every land
The work of an Almighty hand.

Soon as the evening shades prevail,
The moon takes up the wondrous tale,
And nightly to the listening earth
Repeats the story of her birth;
While all the stars that round her burn,
And all the planets in their turn,
Confirm the tidings as they roll,
And spread the truth from pole to pole.
Forever singing, as they shine,
"The hand that made us is divine."

Father G. Ellard, in his book *Christian Life and Worship*, remarks: "Under the hands of the Church, all nature becomes a 'Lift up your heart' and a 'Bless ye the Lord.' Everywhere she makes men see God and she fills the whole world with His charm and radiance."

God rules the world. See him in the beauty of creation; see the order in the world with its laws, the earth in its revolutions, the planets in their orbits. Review the vastness of creation so that your soul may expand with God. The universe has a language, which, though silent, is eloquent.

Only through creatures do we come to know and love God. Only through creatures can we serve God. Hence the need of creatures. I must use creatures in order to attain to God. It was for this purpose God made creatures and filled the earth with them.

In Psalm 103 we read: "The earth shall be filled with the fruit of thy works; bringing forth grass for cattle, and herbs for the service of man; that thou mayst bring bread out of the earth; and that wine may cheer the heart of man. . . .

"He made the moon for seasons; the sun knows his going down. Thou has appointed darkness, and it is night; the sun rises, and man shall go forth to his work, and to his labor until the evening.

"How great are thy works, O Lord! Thou hast made all things in wisdom; the earth is filled with thy riches. So is the great sea which stretches wide its arms. There the ships shall go. All expect of thee that thou give them food in season. What thou givest them, they shall gather up when thou openest thy hand. They shall all be filled with good."

From the majestic Teton Mountains of Wyoming to the smiling pansy in your flower box, there is wonder and mystery. Every moment of our lives we dwell in God's wonder world. If we see not the magic, the fault must be our own.

Contemplating the vast scintillating depths of the midnight sky arched over and around him, Abraham Lincoln said, "I can see how it might be possible for a man to look down upon the earth and be an atheist, but I cannot conceive how he could look up into the heavens and say there is no God."

St. Bernard of Clairvaux found God in the leaves of the beech trees, and Joyce Kilmer reminds us that only God can make a tree.

The poet Joseph M. Plunkett tells us:

I see his blood upon the rose
And in the stars the glory of his eyes,

His body gleams amid eternal snows,
His tears fall from the skies.

I see his face in every flower;
The thunder and the singing of the birds
Are but his voice — and carven by his power
Rocks are his written words.

When spring comes skipping over the hills on tulip-sandaled feet, beauty takes you by the hand and leads you through cool dells where violets blossom like stars and daffodils are sparkling suns.

As you stand in the valley, which throbs with wave upon wave of color, and light, and fragrance, you slip in close to God, having come to him by the old, swift avenue of beauty.

My mother took special delight in the unspoiled beauty of flowers. To her they were symbols of innocence, honor, beauty, and glory. They made music out of color and sang of the duty and lovableness of God.

Each lilac, each tulip, each petunia, for Mother, was a cheerful messenger in living color to speak of God's beauty and kindness. Each May, when spring came leaping over the garden fence, Mother delighted in the rainbow-splashed tulips. With heads erect, as straight and tall as if by some proud monarch sent, the tulips marched along her garden wall, a gold and crimson regiment, the first troopers to invade the yard after the long siege of winter.

If there were sermons in stones and books in babbling brooks — so thought Mother — there were odes and elegies in flowers.

To Mother, flowers were the thoughts of God. It was God who shaped the fragile beauty of the rose, the open-faced loveliness of a pansy, and the enduring simplicity of a geranium.

Our God is a God of joy, of happiness, of love. You

catch the tinkle of his voice in the laughter of a stream. You hear his footsteps in the measured cadence of the bolero. You hear the echo of his joy in the lighthearted music of Mendelssohn. You sense his grandeur in the climactic thunders of Beethoven. You experience his lovableness in the waltzes of Strauss. You thrill to his majesty in the epic symphonies of Bach, Beethoven, and Brahms.

Great men have given their lives to music. Mozart found in music a magic mirror for his own soaring spirit. The haunting, melancholic music of Liszt gleams with flickering flames of gypsy campfires. Brahms' "Lullaby" captures the magic of a child's world balanced on faith and warmed in the glow and radiance of a mother's love.

Music consists of sound poems in which some hear the tread of ancient folklore, some the beat of the sea, some the passion of the gale, and others the voice of some soaring thing that will not stay imprisoned.

There Is Mystery and Beauty All Around Us!

The more we look around, the more we see to admire. From pulsing stars to pushing seeds; from suns of island universes in the sea of God's immensity to unseen atoms holding all the might of unimagined power, there is mystery throbbing everywhere.

We do not live by bread alone, but by the glory of the sky at dawn, the majesty of snowcapped mountains, the flashing silver of a mountain stream, the song of the lark, the rustle of tall corn in the breeze, the magic of the maestro's violin, the shimmering beauty of "Clair De Lune," and the dramatic roll of Ravel's "Bolero."

In an ancient Norse fairy tale, you must travel far and wide beyond seven seas and seven billowing ridges to reach the golden castle of your dreams.

To view the treasures of the universe, however, all you have to do is lift your eyes to the sky. Stars that dot the evening sky glitter like jewels of Indian princes or diamonds from South African mines.

Look up into the Milky Way and see stars poised pale on the fringes of space and gathering fire in frail, pink flames. Over your head swings the "drinking cup" of the heavens, the Big Dipper.

Flung in generous handfuls across the velvet black of night are gems dazzling beyond even Sinbad's most fabulous dreams. There is bright Algol, beloved of camel drivers; then there is Vega, the pale sapphire. Mighty Rigel blazes with bluish-white, a jewel made for a king! Betelgeuse glows moody as an opal, while lovely Aldebaran blossoms like a pale ruby in the distant sky.

That golden blur of light shimmering just south of overhead is the Pleiades, the seven sisters of heaven, sending forth a soft, sweet radiance. Many a night you may have seen the Pleiades rising through the mellow shade, then glitter like a swarm of fireflies caught in a silver braid.

From rim to rim, across the bowl of the sky, glimmers the star-studded haze called the Milky Way, that ribbon of light woven of flaming suns.

The Stars Are a Gift From God

As you look up at the stars, you can say, "You are mine. For us God made these sentinels in the sky. Our Father who is in heaven spread out the dazzling beauty of the Milky Way to speak his message of love."

Tremendous as are the vast bulks of whirling suns that speed down the printless paths of time, they are but grains of sand to him who weighs them in the palm of his hand, poises them in their sweeping orbits, and balances their massive weights as easily as dust beams dancing in the sunlight.

As you gaze out into incomprehensible distances, let your heart leap with love. Send your thoughts racing out through the voids of space, vaulting over the Milky

Way, and dashing over the most distant galaxies observable with the Hubble Space Telescope until you come at last to the great white throne of God.

The universe was made for this purpose only: to speak a message of love. So much does God desire the love of your heart that all the far-flung orbits of the planets, all the vast bulk of mountains and distant stars, all the harmony of the spheres, all the galaxies throbbing overhead — all these are but a slight price for him to pay for your love.

Every moment of our lives we breathe, stand, or move in the temple of God, for the whole universe is that temple. We see the imprint of his hand in all creation.

Each day a bit of magic is waiting for you: a charming love letter from God folded away in unsuspecting places. You will find love letters in the forest at dusk when the trees are all in shadow and filled with indescribable colors. You will find them in the patient prairie that sweeps out beyond little towns and loses itself in immensely distant horizons.

When darkness wraps its mantle of silence around the shoulders of the world, a wizard moon steps out behind a mountaintop to orchestrate a soft ballet of moonbeams on a silver lake. Then, with warm importunate hands the moon looses night's jeweled scarf and flings her loveliness across the sky. Caressingly the moon brushes back the twilight's cloud-soft hair, leaving a gentle kiss upon its brow.

As you continue to gaze at "that orbed maiden with white fire laden, whom mortals call the moon," you suddenly find yourself afloat on an ocean of epic grandeur. Then, silently, one by one, in the infinite meadows of heaven, blossom the lovely stars, the forget-me-nots of the angels. As you look, you know you are honored to be witness of so much majesty, you thrill to know that God is writing you a love letter.

Every season of life reveals a beauty of its own. The

simplest works of nature proclaim the grandeur of the universe and the miracle of life. Nature's gentle beauty whispers softly to our hearts. How precious our moments of quiet communion with the world when the soul reawakens to the wonder of life! We should open our eyes to the treasures that lie at the heart of each beautiful day.

No doubt you have experienced in your life moments when the God of creation moved in close and momentarily touched you with his presence through some natural happening. It might have been something as simple and lovely as a tree standing tall and solitary, reaching up to the heavens from a windswept plain. It might have been an ocean shore with the waves crashing in with tireless power and majesty. It might have been a spring day with its sweet promise of fresh life after the exhaustion of winter.

'For Anyone Who Is Lonely. . .'

Among the fifty thousand victims of the Nazi death camp at Bergen-Belsen was the young Dutch girl Anne Frank. Her diary of the days she spent hiding from the Nazis in Amsterdam inspired millions of people after her death. The following item from her diary is worth quoting here: "For anyone who is lonely, or unhappy, or worried, the best thing is to go somewhere he can be alone, alone with the sky, with nature, and with God. For it is only then that man feels that all is as it should be and that God wants us to be happy in a simple, beautiful world. As long as this is so — and it always will be so — I know that in every circumstance there is a comfort; I believe firmly that nature makes so much of our sorrow lighter."

Love comes to the one who loves; beauty comes to the seekers of beauty. As you experience wonder, marvelous things happen around you and within you. The manifest unity of things, the laws and regularities of the universe, the rhythm of the seasons, the fertility of the soil, the concordances of sound and color, and, above all, the persistence of a sense of the sacred at all times — all these things keep wonder alive.

Ask of the bright worlds around us as they roll in the everlasting harmony of their circles, and they shall tell you of the Creator whose power launched them on their course. Ask of the mountains that lift their great peaks among and above the clouds, and the snow-capped summit of one shall seem to call aloud to the snow-clad top of another in proclaiming the fact that God laid their foundations from the dawn of creation.

Ask of the ocean's waters, and the roar of their boundless waves shall chant from shore to shore a hymn of benediction to God who said to them: "Hitherto shall ye come, and no further."

Ask of the rivers, and as they roll onward to the sea they bear ceaseless tribute to the everlasting power of God who struck open their fountains and poured them down through the valleys.

Let us now ponder these lines by Edna St. Vincent Millay:

O God, I cried, no dark disguise
Can e'er hereafter hide from me
Thy radiant identity.
Thou canst not move across the grass
But my quick eyes will see Thee pass. . .
I know the path that tells Thy way
Through the cool eve of every day.
God, I can push the grass apart
And lay my finger on Thy heart.

Father Jack Wintz, O.F.M., would have us keep in mind that praise is the bubbling-over of the Spirit. Surely, one of our deepest human instincts is adoration, and we do well to let the Spirit flow freely through us in words of praise. The "Our Father" recognizes this in its first exclamation: "Hallowed be thy name!"

Praise takes us from our self-preoccupation and leads us outward to God and to the creation that bears his imprint. According to Franciscan author Murray Bodo, this is the key to the prayer of St. Francis of Assisi. Like St. Francis, the Spirit prompts us to celebrate our brotherhood or sisterhood with other creatures and to praise God, not in isolation from creation, but through sunlight, rain, wind, and flowers.

May our reaction to all these gifts of God be that of George Herbert:

Thou that has given so much to me,
Give one thing more — a grateful heart;
Not thankful when it pleaseth me,
As if thy blessings had spare days,
But such a heart whose pulse may be
Thy praise.

In her book *Gift From the Sea*, Anne Morrow Lindbergh informs us that once she was vacationing in a cottage on a lonely beach. As she looked at the pelicans, gulls, and sandpipers soaring and circling around her, she felt "melted into the universe, lost in it, as one is lost in a canticle of praise swelling from an unknown crowd in a cathedral: 'Praise ye the Lord, all ye fishes of the sea — all ye birds of the air — praise ye the Lord!' "

Sometimes when you stand in awe before a lovely scene, the soothing atmosphere physically envelops you, gently leading you to new levels of understanding. It's as if your body becomes an extrasensory receiver and you somehow experience the colors, smells, textures, and what lies beyond, as each sense is sharpened to an exquisite pitch.

Slowly, you melt into the scene, becoming at once

154

participant and spectator. Afterward, although time has passed, the sensation lingers, stored as a prized cassette you can replay at will.

The 'Smiling Pope'

Pope John Paul I was known as the "Smiling Pope." Without hesitation he told the world how he prayed: "Personally, when I speak alone with God, I prefer to feel myself a child. I abandon myself to the spontaneous tenderness that a child has for his mama and papa.

"To be before God as I am in reality, with all my misery and with the best of myself; to let rise to the surface from the depths of my being the child I once was, who wants to laugh, to chatter, to love the Lord, and who sometimes feels the need to cry so that he may be shown mercy — all this helps me to pray."

Archbishop Rembert G. Weakland of Milwaukee has a beautiful prayer: "Loving God, let me find your presence in all things, not just in the glamorous and overwhelming events, but in the daily chores and tasks, in all your people — in the good and the struggling, in the healed and in those in need.

"Loving God, help me to learn to accept and to cherish now these little bits of joy, of light, of sunshine, of goodness, of friendship, so that when the long and seemingly interminable winter days of life oppress, they, too, will be embraced as your blessings."

"Prayer," said Mother Angelica, "isn't just a handful of eloquent phrases or holy verse. It isn't only a cry for help or a plea for forgiveness. Prayer is the lifting of our hearts and minds to God. For no matter what we're saying, we're asking, 'Do You love me?' And no matter how God answers, the answer is 'Yes, I do.' "

With Liam Brophy you may wish to pray, "Thankful praise to Thee, O Lord, for everything, from tiny to tremendous, from the height of dazzling heavens to the utmost dark of ocean depths."

High up on the snow-covered Adamello Mountains in northern Italy, on July 16, 1988, Pope John Paul II said Mass 10,300 feet above sea level. He preached communion with God through communion with nature.

He said it was a message humanity needs to absorb if it is to have spiritual peace and peace among nations.

"The mountains," the Holy Father related during the Mass, "always have had a special fascination for my soul," explaining that they invite humanity "to be uplifted, not only materially, but spiritually."

The Pope then went on to say that the beauty of the mountains is a sign that "nature is a perpetual hymn to the greatness of the Creator, and an invitation to submerge yourself in prayer."

The Holy Father noted how famous religious figures, starting with Moses on Mount Sinai, had their divine dialogue at spots of natural beauty: "In the splendor of nature, the Creator manifests his beauty, and puts at the disposal of humanity enormous resources which should be used in an orderly way to obtain the ultimate end inherent in human beings."

Pope John Paul II would agree with the words of the poet S. Omar Barker:

> Reason it out if you feel you must:
> Mountains are only chunks of crust
> Heaved from the depths in primal stress,
> Owning no power to curse or bless:
> Yet something about God's patterned gift
> Of timbered mountains gives a lift
> Unto the soul who sees in them
> Nature's holy diadem.
> Unto the peaks so near God's skies,
> I shall ever lift mine eyes!

My first adventure into the high places of the Alps left me breathless with wonder and admiration. On the morning of Tuesday, August 23, 1960, I left Lucerne, Switzerland, and traveled by coach and cable car to the top of Mount Trubsee. All around me majestic mountains leaped to the sky, like *Saturn V* rockets. The air entered my lungs like a rapture. I exhaled it in a canticle of praise to the Maker of all good days, and of this day in particular.

The words I had said at the beginning of Mass that morning took on fresh meaning, like words heard for the first time: "Send forth your light and your truth. They have led me and brought me into your holy mountain and into your tabernacle."

Truly, this was a holy spot. Here, indeed, all of nature sings of God. The very rocks seemed to echo the words of Psalm 100: "Sing joyfully to God, all the earth; serve ye the Lord with gladness. Come in before his presence with exceeding great joy."

Here was happiness and delight. Here the vision of a day that would remain forever bright and shining. I could not add one word to all the lyric lines that tell the story of this mystic land.

First Sioux Priest

In June 1985 Father Collins Jordan became the first native American to be ordained a priest for the Diocese of Rapid City, South Dakota. Father Jordan is a descendant of the famous Chief Red Cloud of the Oglala Sioux and of Chief Hollow Horn Bear of the Brulé Sioux.

"To American Indians," said Father Jordan, "all of Mother Earth is considered sacred. All physical laws and forces and manifestations are from God. God is present and works on our behalf in and through visible, material realities. The spiritual heritage of Indians reveals a sacramental vision. Indians see the religious values of their tradition as still valid in their Christian faith.

"The true Indian sees the divine presence in the

whole world of nature. Religion is a part of his entire life. He does not put it into a compartment as modern technological man does."

Father Ted Zuern, S.J., agrees with this outlook. Father Zuern is a Jesuit who has worked for more than thirty years among the Indians. According to Father Zuern, Indians never lost the feeling of mystery and awe associated with the universe.

In addition to Indians' reverence for all creation, Father Zuern cited the importance to Indians of the extended family, the great sense of community, and the respect and love for older generations. The idea of family was, and is, paramount.

"Also important," said Father Zuern, "is the Indians' sense that prayer is proper at all times. They had a sense, no matter what they were doing, of giving thanks. There was a living with a sense of the Creator at all times. And there was a relationship there between the Creator and themselves."

John Grim, who is an authority on Indian life, assures us that perhaps no religious value of American Indians is so obvious to outsiders as their sense of beauty, displayed not so much in particular forms, such as dancing or singing, but rather in the human spontaneity that performs them.

Indian rituals hold a mirror of beauty to the earth itself. Whether danced in the Kachina cycles of the Southwestern peoples or in the Sun Dance of the Plains peoples, the repetitive act is valued as beautiful because it enters into the recurrent forces of the earth and evokes them.

By making such ritual statements of great beauty and drama, Indians believe that they are promoting long life and happiness both for individuals and for the people. Beauty reaches into the inner form of the human, harmonizing it with the forces of the earth that gave it life.

Thanks to the kindness of Barbara Tippery, I can share her poem with you:

Seek not to see God with your eyes. . .
The dazzling light would blind you.
Seek Him instead in calm blue skies
And His creations all around you.

See His Beauty in fields of flowers. . .
His Strength in the pounding surf,
His Joy in golden morning hours,
His Richness in all the earth.

See His Greatness in mountains high. . .
His Warmth in a soft summer wind,
His Eternity in the star-filled sky. . .
His Promise when a new day begins.

See His Love in a mother's smile. . .
Wisdom in an old man's eyes,
His Innocence in a newborn child. . .
And His Hope in a lover's sighs.

Keep in mind the words of Martin H. Padovani, who tells us, "There are three important lessons Jesus teaches us: God always loves us, God always forgives us, God is always present with us. Religion is supposed to bring us peace, joy, hope, comfort, and consolation. If it doesn't, then something is wrong with us — not with our religion or faith."

The poet Ralph Spaulding Chusham caught the thrill of living with God in these words:

Oh, the sheer joy of it,
Living with Thee,
God of the universe,
Lord of a tree,

Maker of mountains,
Lover of me!

I would like to conclude this book with a statement from Father John Catoir, the director of The Christophers: "My favorite quote is from Juliana of Norwich, a fifteenth-century English mystic who wrote: 'The greatest honor you can give Almighty God, greater than all your sacrifices and mortifications, is to live gladly because of the knowledge of His love.' This thought has given me a whole new perspective in living my faith. It's helped me to freshen my prayer with joy."